The

Old Pubs

Of

Lichfield

by
John Shaw

"The Old Pubs of Lichfield"

Published by George Lane Publishing
Lichfield, Staffs
WS13 6 DU

First published March 2001
Printed by WM Print, Walsall
WS2 9NE

ISBN 0-9539868-0-2

Acknowledgements

My grateful thanks go to the following friends and Citizens of the City who have given me so much help and support enabling me to produce this little tome on a subject that is of interest to many people in Lichfield. The list is far from complete as so many pieces of information were passed to me without any names being offered. I do, however, thank them for their kindness and interest in this book.

Ted Ashley (for much original collation and shared information of pub names at the start of the research)

Michael Dace (Lichfield Librarian at the start of my research for giving me so much help with the initial recording of pub names in Lichfield).

John Sanders (kind permission to reproduce colour slides and photographs of the 60s)

Local Studies Section (Lichfield Libraries) for their kind help and assistance and also kind permission to reproduce some of their local photograph collection)

The late Ena Millard of Beacon Street (information and photographs)

Cuthbert Brown (author of Born in a Cathedral City and use of photographs of Beacon Street)

Ralph James (James Redshaw Limited of Dam Street, for his advice, proof reading and encouragement)

Lichfield Heritage Collection (permission to use photographs from the collection at St Mary's Centre)

Godfrey Eland (proof reading and good advice)

Steve Lees of Stowe Street (photograph of the Ring of Bells and information on Stowe Street)

Friends at WM Print, Walsall, (for their help in the preparation of this book)

The late Jim Tonks of Stowe Street (for his information of the 1930s and 40s and photographs)

THE FATAL SHOOTING CASE AT
THE GRESLEY ARMS INN.

An inquest was held on Wednesday evening at the Gresley Arms Inn, before Mr. Charles Simpson, city coroner, on the body of Samuel Bates, labourer, of Walsall, who was shot dead on Tuesday night by William George Green, landlord of the above inn.

The body having been viewed, the first witness called was Henry Joseph Stych a lad, living next door to the Gresley Arms Inn, whose testimony was given in such a manner as to be hardly intelligible. He was understood to mean that shortly after eight o'clock William G. Green came to his house and asked for the gun which be had previously been using. He loaded the gun in Green's presence, charging it with powder and paper, and then handed it to him. He then proceeded to the Gresley Arms Inn, it being then about twenty minutes after eight. He went into the front kitchen, where there were three strangers besides the deceased, who was standing on one side of the fireplace. Mrs. Stych was also in the kitchen. William Green followed.

…Mr. Walmesley: What about the marble that was in this gun?-Witness: I did not know that there was one. Well then you did not put a marble in it? -- No sir. What had you been doing with this gun?--I had been letting it off.

Mr. Mason : Cannot you swear positively that you did not put anything in the gun besides the powder and paper? – I pulled a piece of paper out of my pocket; there was no marble in it. Was there any hard substance in the paper ? -- I had bits of cork in my pocket. There might have been bits of them.

Mr. Walmesley: What was the cause of you charging the gun? -- Green asked me to charge it. He said he would let it off to frighten those in the front kitchen. Did you see deceased picked up? -- I did not; I went for the doctor.

George Cotton, bricklayer, living at 41 Ball Street, Walsall said he knew Samuel Bates. He came with him, James Ellson, and Edward Plummer, from Walsall to Lichfield on Tuesday morning to work. After finishing they came to lodge at the Gresley Arms Inn. They made the acquaintance of William G. Green. Witness sat on a chair beside the fire, whilst the deceased stood with his back to the fire. The deceased was stooping down, and whilst speaking to witness he dropped down dead. Witness exclaimed " Good Gad, he is shot." Green said "There is nothing in the gun but powder, he cannot be hurt." Witness never saw the gun. After the occurrence Green sent at once for the superintendent and the doctors.

Mr Walmesley: Do you know what motive he had for firing that gun off?-- No sir.

Mrs. Fanny Stych said she lived next door to Mr Green. She saw William G. Green come in carrying a gun in his hand. The gun seemed to catch against the iron bar that supports the screen, and exploding put out the gas.

Mr. Walmesley: I suppose it was merely a lark to frighten them?- That was all, sir.

Mr. Neeld: Have you seen any marbles about the house ?-That is a question I cannot answer.

Mr. Neeld: That question ought to he answered, sir.

Witness : I have no marbles in my house.

Several immaterial questions were afterwards put to witness, but she declined to answer them, and becoming rude and refractory, she was ultimately dismissed.

William George Green on his oath, said he went to Stych's house, and told Henry Joseph Stych to put a small charge into the gun. He saw him load it. He saw him put about half a charge of powder in it. He saw him put paper on the top of it. With that he went by the fire, and lit his pipe. He took the gun and walked into the Gresley Arms Inn. As he was going through the passage, intending to fire the gun in the back kitchen, the muzzle of the gun came against the iron bar which supports the screen, and exploded.

Witness (in anguish): I never thought of shooting anybody.

Mr Pearsall: No one for a moment thinks that.

In reply to further questions from the jury. witness said that being the 5th of November he said, "Joe, put a small charge of powder in, and I'll go and let it off in the back kitchen to frighten them."

George William Homan, surgeon, Lichfield, said he was called to deceased about 25 minutes to nine. He came at once and found the deceased lying on the floor of the kitchen. He was quite dead. On examination, witness found a wound on the left temple, just about the eyebrow. This wound fractured and penetrated the skull, admitting his finger as far as be could get it into the substance of the brain. He made a *post-mortem* examination of the head, where he found the marble produced which caused death.

After conversation amongst the jurors, Mr. Pearsall said he thought they should have the position in which the gun was when it exploded more clearly shown, and also the charge which was put into the gun more clearly defined.

The jurors then went with William George Green to the scene of the occurrence, where he showed and explained to them how it happened.

The jury returned to the court apparently satisfied on that point.

Mr. Simpson in summing up said the evidence was quite clear as to the manner in which the deceased came to his death; and Green was doing nothing unlawful when the gun exploded, and it appeared he was in amity with all parties in the house, and there was no disturbance in the house. Were they satisfied that the gun went off accidentally, then it was an ordinary verdict of accidental death, and that would be their judgement.

Mr. Neeld: Supposing it could he proved that the lad did put the marble in the gun.

Mr. Simpson: Then I do not know that it would make the least difference.

Mr. Oakley It would clear the mystery.

Mr. Simpson remarked that were they satisfied the gun went off by accident, it was of no consequence by whom it was let off.

The jury then returned a verdict of "Accidental death," believing at the same time that Henry Joseph Stych knew something about the marble

As reported in the Lichfield Mercury 8th November 1878

Contents – Streets and Maps

Contents – General

Explanation of Typesetting styles of Pub names

Pubs, that are closed or demolished   **The Old Crown**
Pubs still open   *George the Fourth* *

The Abbot of Burton brewed good ale,
on Fridays when they fasted –
but the Abbot of Burton
ne'er tasted his own
as long as his neighbours'
lasted

An old rhyme

Preface

This book is the result of my interest in "The Old Pubs" from listening to elderly Lichfeldians ruminating on the lost pubs of their youth. My research aided by many friends culminated in the creation of a slide show, illustrating the pubs, the buildings and the sites, and an ever-increasing number of old photographs. I have over the last six years presented the slide show and talk to many varied groups and organisations around the City.

The interest and the enthusiasm shown for the subject and the often-repeated question *Are you going to do a book?* has helped me to attempt this publication. It is not intended to be a detailed history of the subject - I will leave that to the learned historians - but a printed version of my slide show.

Pubs are unique places and we are privileged to have them for the benefits they can bestow on our lives. Each has a personality of its own, its own character and reputation indeed we often refer to them as we do to human friends. They provide not only fellowship but the meeting place for many organisations and groups within our community; a well run English pub with good ale and good company can provide us all with amusement and sustenance. Sadly, as time moves on, they are rapidly dwindling. If you have a good local then you are fortunate indeed, my friend.

I have for clarity included various maps circa 1902 of the streets which have been re-developed over the last 30 years, and again for the same reason not included any pubs which have been built since 1946, unless they were old pubs moved for re-development such as the Bald Buck on Greenhill.

Lastly, I hope that I may be forgiven for getting things wrong or leaving something out. The possibility that I can be mistaken has not escaped me; I am only too pleased to receive suggestions or information on the subject. I lay no claim to being a local historian, though this brief account is my small offering to the rich history of our City.

JOHN SHAW
Lichfield
2001

All bar one

Strolling into Lichfield one morning in the company of the **Prince of Wales, Duke of York, Duke of Wellington, Earl of Lichfield** and **Lord Rodney**, we saw by the light of the **Seven Stars, Little George** picking up **Acorns** from under the **Royal Oak**, and the little **Turks Head** was decorated with **Feathers**, picked up from near the **Fountain** after being cast off by the **Swan**, and his brother **George** carrying a **Malt Shovel**, walking to the **Railway** via the **Trent Valley Hotel** for the purpose of unloading **Three Tuns** which, after being weighed correctly on the **Scales**, were to be taken and **Spread Eagled** on the **Bowling Green**.

Going further into the City, we asked for the **Crossed Keys** and entered the **Castle**, where we saw **George the Fourth** who had put on one of his **Old Crowns** for the purpose of seeing a fight between **George and Dragon**. Sitting by his side we could just see the **Queen's Head** and in her hair was the **Staffordshire Knot**, and also visible was **Levetts Arms** around her. After the fight we proceeded over the **Bridge** towards the **Smithfield**, where we were overtaken by a **Greyhound** chasing through the **Bluebell** wood where we came across **Robin Hood** and his favourite **Horse and Jockey**, who by the way, was drinking at the **King's Head** while his master, taking cover behind a **Holly Bush** was undecided whether to let fly at a **Bald Buck** running past or a **Goat's Head** which had come into sight.

Evening arrived and the expert samplers being defeated as to which house supplied the best beer and where civility was best served, the **Angel** of this trip decided to go with the **Marquis of Anglesey**, who being tired, tripped and was prevented from falling by the strong **Carpenter's Arms**. The visit was brought to an end by a game of **Chequers**.

Who knows the author of this parody on Lichfield pubs? It was found by a Mrs Murphy a resident of Wade Street, amongst her mother's documents. Unfortunately there was no other information with it. It was probably composed in the mid 1930s as it refers to Pubs still open in Lichfield in 1939.

One pub open at that time and not listed is the Three Crowns. Two more that are now considered to be within the City boundaries are the Constitution and the Shoulder of Mutton. The latter was for some years known as Freeford.

Introduction

The subject of drink was the major talking point in the early part of the nineteenth century; indeed some 43% of the Government's revenue came from duty on alcohol. The nation's middle classes were stirred into action in that period with the famous engravings of Hogarths "Gin Alley". The Government of the day with the Duke of Wellington as the Prime Minister were moved to place duty on the *"Cheap Gin"* of the day and to popularise Beer as a *wholesome* drink; this resulted in the passing of the 1830 Beer Act which allowed any private householder on the payment of Two Pounds to have a Beer only licence. This was the start of what we now call the *"Public House"*. So much terminology is obtained from those early beer houses – **Best Room** or **Lounge** (the better room for the more up market clients), **Bar** (the bar which prevented the customers from intruding into the private part of the house - the counter idea came in later in the century), **Smoke Room** (a room set aside for the cigar or pipe smokers of the day), **Tap Room** (the room where the barrels were stored and beer tapped).

In the three months following this act some 24,342 licences were issued, Lichfield no doubt having its share. Most of these beerhouses were disorderly and unhygienic, the *wholesome* beer did not stop the drunkenness of the day and in an attempt to put it right, the Government in 1834 introduced a second Act which divided the licence into three parts; the full publican's licence was granted annually, as it is today, and the beerhouses were divided into "on" and "off" sales. In 1869 and 1872 further legislation came into force and with the Temperance Movement gaining ground, all drinking establishments came under the wing of the Licensing Magistrates, who then took the opportunity to close down many poorly run pubs. This caused the Brewers who, up to that point, were content to sell their beer direct to the independent pub, to buy up licensed premises in an attempt to gain outlets for their products.

Lichfield along with many towns had a high ratio of pubs to population. To perhaps illustrate this point the following figures are illuminating.

1732 population	3,500	80 pubs	1 to 44	people
1834 population	5,000	72 pubs	1 to 69	people
1900 population	8,000	52 pubs	1 to 163	people
1936 population	8,500	46 pubs	1 to 184	people

The figure for 1732 is recorded in various histories of the time, the figure for 1834 is more accurate as by that date the local Trade Directories had been produced. The City area has a population of some 30,000 today, with approx 26 pubs (not including wine bars). To achieve that same ratio of 1 to 69, Lichfield City area would need about **434** pubs, a mind blowing thought.

There were strictly three kinds of licensed premises during the era of Lichfield's golden age of pubs: **Inns** which had a full licence for beer, wine and spirits, also providing accommodation, **Taverns** which had a full licence, beer, wine and spirits and **Beerhouses** which served beer only. For the purpose of this book we shall refer to all kinds of premises by the modern term of **"Pub"**. The pilgrimage era, the coaching era and the position of Lichfield on two main roads had an affect on the large number of pubs in the City. They started to reduce in number mainly due to economic forces and the two world wars, which saw a number close, due to a lack of business and shortage of supplies.

9

*There is nothing which has yet
been contrived by man,
by which so much happiness
is produced as by a good
tavern or inn*

Samuel Johnson
21 March 1776

The Old Crown

A pub with a long history and some recent folklore, the pub is first listed in 1781 being marked on Snape's map of 1780. The Old Crown was a busy point during the coaching era. It was purchased by the Lichfield Brewery Company in 1879 and up to that time possessed a fair amount of stabling and yard. It had a number of rooms, the most famous being its Market Room in which deals were made and prices haggled. It was a listed building and at its closure and re-building into a retail unit it sadly fell down in the night. It was of course re-built as it is to-day, in the same style and shape, as an optician and shoe shops. The photograph shows the archway which in its last years was used by various traders, a well-remembered pub to many people in Lichfield to-day.

George the Fourth *

Deeds in the Lichfield record office record the sale of part of these premises to the County Constabulary in 1851. The deeds state that the George the Fourth, known previously as the **Old Goat's Head** and the **Old Golden Ball** stands on a very historic site, the pub at that time being held by Thomas Stringer who we see has a brother running the Old Golden Ball in Tamworth Street in 1850, no doubt the Stringer family keeping the name Old Golden Ball in the family. It would appear that during the years when the police station occupied part of the George the Fourth, it did keep operating as a pub, Thomas Stringer being listed as landlord through many of the years until the move of the Police into the Guildhall in 1889.

The Police used rooms and buildings at the rear of the pub which appear still to exist and are used by the pub; they had rear access to Wade Street, Guildhall and the Courts.

A pub has stood on this site since before the 1750s (no doubt probably pre dating that). It is still open today and thriving. The photo shows the view down Bore Street and the George the Fourth before it had its *"Brewery Tudor"* facing. The Guildhall, Donegal House and the Tudor Café remain unchanged.

Bore Street continued

11

The Dolphin

The **Dolphin** was listed in 1818 under the name of Henry Genders a name we will see in Birmingham Road as he ran two pubs in that area. The Dolphin was an interesting pub,

The building being tiered construction and was for many years a pub from which a large number of carriers operated . The Daintys operated to Barton and Burton daily, the Wheatcrofts operated wagons daily to Bristol & West and to Leeds and the North.

The photograph shows the Dolphin circa 1896. The last landlord listed is a Percy Woodfield whom we see some years later running the Lemon Tree in Beacon Street. The Building was demolished in 1912 and the present building erected in 1913 for the Co-op as which it continued to around the late 1980s, when it went for a Burton) a Burton's shop, I might add).

The Goat's Head

The Goat's Head originally stood not in Bore Street but just down Breadmarket Street (see photo under Breadmarket St). It was rebuilt on the corner site some three storeys

high. The building was refaced when it was converted into its present use as Barclays Bank.

The photograph shows the pub around the mid-60s looking down Breadmarket Street. The old Goats Head stood approx where the archway of the pub is, and rebuilt on the corner site around the turn of the century. A well remembered pub it was also for many years the HQ of Lichfield Rugby Club.

The pub closed 9th January 1970. The earliest landlord known is William Hobday in 1811. From 1834 to 1880 it was run by Margaret Slater, a period of some 46 years.

Woolpack

Listed in 1793, it lasted up to 1904, the last recorded landlord being George Culveswell, 1899 to 1904. It was then converted to retail use and now forms part of Salloway's the Jewellers. A carrier is mentioned running from the Woolpack to West Bromwich and Walsall in the mid 1860s. Among the wonderful English names you find in research of the old Lichfield pubs is Jethro Scoffham who was the licensee 1861 to 1870.

Bore Street continued

Prince of Wales (Turf Tavern/Queen's Head) *

This pub was originally named the **Queen's Head** listed in 1818 to Thomas Whitehouse and 1830 to 1834 George Sharman. It would appear that the name then moved to the newly erected pub in Queen Street, this pub then taking the name **Turf Tavern,** under which name it continued until 1867 under the management of William and Thomas Riley. The pub then became the Prince of Wales from 1868 and started its thirty years under the management of the Ffrench family, long associated with the Lichfield pub history.

Recent years have seen the pub operate under the name **Pipers,** it becoming a piano bar and in late 2000 having a late licence, becoming some kind of nightclub.
As the Prince of Wales it became the meeting place of many Lichfield organisations through the years.

The photograph shows the **Prince of Wales** in the 1900s looking down Bore Street. The buildings on the right have not changed but the left side has been mostly rebuilt down to what is now Kim's Kabin.

The above photograph shows the view from the reverse angle, with the **Prince of Wales** on the left and the Clock Tower before its demolition and the opening up of the new Friary Road in the 1920s, a much altered view. On the right hand corner is Jones' Garage, which as we will see in the Bird Street page, was the original building that housed the **Talbot.**

13

Breadmarket is a short street with only two pubs listed there during the years, the **Old Goat's Head** and the **Three Crowns** of Samuel Johnson fame. The two following photographs show both in their working days. The Three Crowns is now part of the Estate Agents premises.

Three Crowns

This famous old pub frequented by Dr. Johnson appears on Snape's map of 1781. In 1793 to 1859 two members of the Cato family ran the Inn for a period of some 78 years, 1793 to 1834 by Joseph and from 1834 to 1859 by John Joseph, his son. Dr Samuel Johnson visited Lichfield on a fairly regular basis, during his later years always staying at the Three Crowns just yards from his birthplace. The Three Crowns, sometimes listed as being in Market Place was during Johnson's time a very busy and important Inn.

The last known landlord was John Barber in 1940. The name of Three Crowns relates to the union of the Three Kingdoms under James the First; an earlier version of the name is a reference to the Triple Crown of the Papacy.

The Old Goat's Head

This pub is the successor to its previous existence in the premises which became the **George the Fourth** in Bore Street. The pub when listed in Breadmarket Street stood a little further into the street as the photograph shows.

The Old Goat's Head

The Three Crowns

Talbot

Built in 1760 to serve the growing coaching trade it was owned throughout its life by members of the Jackson family. It was built on land owned by the Earls of Shrewsbury, whose family name was Talbot. The Talbot finally closing at the end of the Coaching era with the arrival of railways in Lichfield and the many towns its coaches served. One of the coaches serving the Talbot was *'The Amity'* between Birmingham & Sheffield. At the closure of the Inn it became retail premises and as the photograph shows was at the end of its life a Motor Garage. The photo *right* shows the early 1950s, the lack of traffic contrasting with the present day as we take our lives in our hands crossing over to the Library in the Friary. The site is now occupied with a 1960s shopping development.

Rose & Crown

Now the *Big Fisherman* fish and chip shop, it was listed on Snape's map in 1781 as the **Bear's Head** to James Godwin. In 1793 it has become the **Boar's Head** still being run by the same James Godwin. 1834 sees the first mention of the name **Rose and Crown**, with William Wheatley as landlord; the alley alongside was called Moss's entry and led to Friars Walk and the route through to the Bowling Green Inn. The walk still exists in part and can be used to access the car parks in the Friary. The pub had gone by the First World War as indeed had so many.

George Hotel *

So much has been written about the George Hotel that a brief description seems inadequate; it is first mentioned in 1704, much rebuilt to its present shape around the mid-eighteenth century. Among the many stories of the George is the writing of George Farquhar's *"The Recruiting Officer"* when staying here as a recruiting officer. His best-known play *"Beaux' Stratagem"* has a scene based on the George in Lichfield containing a line' *"I have heard your town of Lichfield is much famed for its ale, I think I'll taste that"*. The George was of course a very important Coaching Inn with stabling for some sixty horses and more at a site in St John Street. It was also the centre of political activity in Lichfield and many stories abound of that period.

Kings Head *

Which King no one is sure. The pub is first mentioned on this site in 1408 as the **Antelope** and standing next to it (on the site of Waits' premises) was an Inn called the **Unicorn;** old maps show the area behind marked as Unicorn Yard. The Kings Head had become so named by 1650. It became an important Inn during the coaching era and also used by many carriers to Birmingham, Uttoxeter and beyond. Of the coaches that plied from the Kings Head were the *"Herald"* to London and Manchester and the *"True Blue"* to Rugeley and Birmingham. Still going strong and a very popular pub in Lichfield.

Bird Street continued

17

Wheatsheaf

Standing next to the Swan, the building still exists today, but as part of the Swan premises. It is first listed in 1818 to Thomas Shrigley, being a very small pub next to the much larger Swan Hotel or Inn as it was. The Wheatsheaf became very much used as the vaults or bar to the Swan. The pub closed just at the start of the First World War, the last landlord being Thomas Andrews. The Author has a token marked "*J. Trevor, Wheatsheaf Inn, Lichfield*" for the amount of **1/-** (one shilling or 5p for our younger readers).

Swan Hotel

Now sadly at the time of writing, it is closed following its use both as a bar and college centre since the late 1980s. The Swan is according to the Victoria County History first mentioned in 1362; it has been much rebuilt through the years and was one of the principal Coaching Inns of Lichfield. In 1535 it is known as the **Lily White Swan.** It is again perhaps inadequate to describe the history of this fine Inn in a few short sentences. Who of those who remember the 1960s and 70s at the Swan can forget that remarkable period when the Swan was **the** meeting place of so many Lichfield organisations and clubs and who can forget the landlord of that period, the late and sadly missed Leo Fanning, probably the best "mine host" in Lichfield for many a long year.

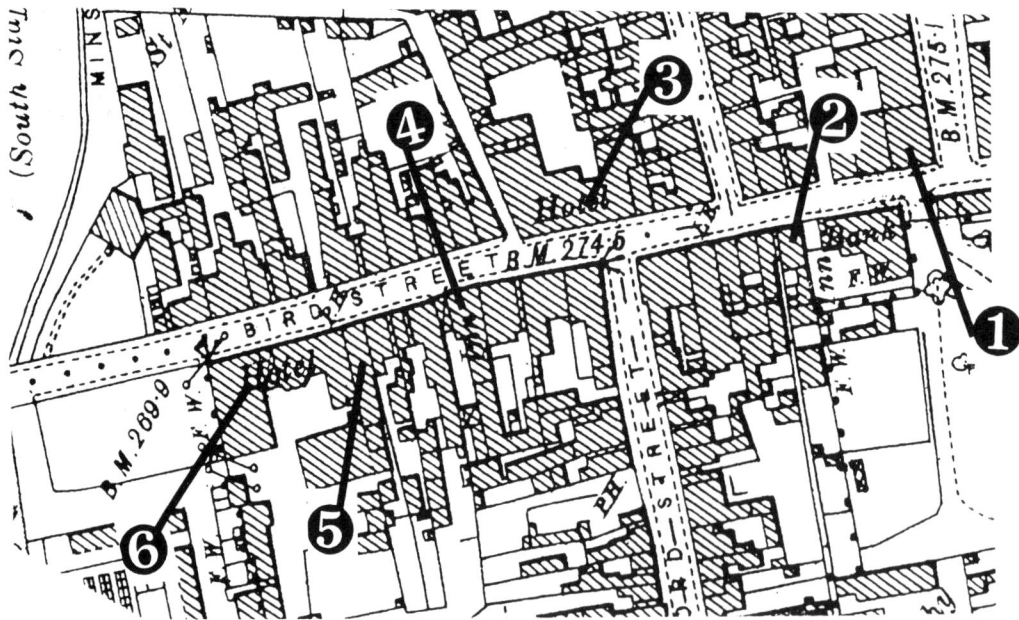

1. Talbot   2. Rose & Crown   3.George Hotel   4. King's Head

5.Wheatsheaf   6.Swan Hotel

Board

Listed as the **Board** in 1830 to Henry Genders, this pub has in recent years been known as Redlock Cottage. The building still exists and is a private house. It served as a beerhouse to the nearby Canal wharfs and limekilns. By the 1850s Henry's wife Hannah had taken over the running and by the middle of the 1850s it had been renamed as the **Spotted Dog** or **Dog** as it was known locally. This of course referred to the Talbot hunting dog and the arms of the Talbots (Earls of Shrewsbury). In 1861 it was being run by Joseph Genders probably the son of Henry and Hannah. By 1869 it had stopped being listed, as Joseph Genders had become the landlord of the nearby **Duke of Wellington,** the pub having reverted to a private residence.

Duke of Wellington *

Recorded in 1818 to Thomas Summerfield whose family ran the Duke until 1868 when the above Joseph Genders had become mine host, it was built to serve the two canal wharves close by. The name is obviously due to the Duke of Wellington's fame at that time. It still continues to serve the local community and is remembered by Lichfield people in pre-war days for the summer walks along the canal towpath from the **Horse and Jockey** at Freeford to the **Duke** and then on up to Pipehill for the last one at the **Royal Oak.**

City Brewery

One of Lichfield's five breweries, built in 1874, it closed after a fire in 1916 and was taken over by the Wolverhampton and Dudley brewery that used it until the 1980s as a Malthouse. Some of the original buildings still remain at the time of writing alongside the railway line to Walsall.

Bowling Green *

Bowls has been played on this site since the 1670s and remarkably still continues. The pub is listed in 1737 but no doubt some kind of beerhouse was there before this. It stood isolated in the Friary area approached by footpaths and a small track. None of the original buildings remain as it was totally rebuilt in the 1930s Roadhouse style. It is remarkable today as being on a traffic island, which came about with the arrival of first the new Friary Road from Bore Street to the Birmingham Road, then the linking of the Birmingham and Walsall Roads until finally, the arrival of the Western by-pass to complete the traffic scheme as it is to-day. For many years in the 50s and 60s it was the main centre for many Dinners and Dances until the new Civic Hall was built. It did change its name for a period to **Monterey Exchange,** (what connection this name had with Lichfield the Lord only knows), but to our relief the original name has been restored and provides a link with 330 years of history for this pub

1. Board/Spotted Dog   2. Duke of Wellington   3. City Brewery

4. Bowling Green Inn

Lamb Inn

The Lamb Inn is marked on Snape's map of 1781. Inns of this name always existed in Cathedral cities and were close to the Cathedral, the name being taken from *"Lamb of God who takest away the sins of the World"*, and very often being owned by the Church. The Lamb was most certainly around some 100 to 150 years before Snape's .map. It is recorded that an Inn called the **Angel** stood in Beacon Street near to the Cathedral gates. Was this the forerunner of the Lamb? The Lamb had gone by the early 1800s.

Coach and Horses

An old Coaching Inn dating back to the time before the Bird Street was widened and it was necessary to go all round Stowe to enter the City from the north. It was the custom until then to unload at this point. The Inn stands down an archway and is now a private house called **Whitehall**. It is listed on the Conduit Lands map of 1766 and was being run by a Thomas Cork in 1834.

George and Dragon *

First listed in 1818 to George Willday it stands next to the tollhouse, which barred the entrance for wheeled traffic entering the city either down Beacon Street or via Gaia Lane.

and so avoiding the tolls. The George & Dragon would have gained business from its position, and the many wagons which would have unloaded at this point, rather than paying the toll.

The Tollhouse is the small white painted House to the right of the George and still exists very little changed. The George & Dragon still serves that part of Lichfield and has that pleasant atmosphere of a country inn.

Little George

1860 sees the earliest listing to Henry Charles; it was run by this gentleman until 1880, and existed as a pub until the outbreak of World War Two under the management of a member of the Hines family, a Joseph Hines. The pub then became once more a private residence and still stands at the corner of Beacon Street and Anson Avenue with some alteration; the licence of this pub was transferred after the War to the new pub in Wheel Lane the **Windmill**.

The Pheasant

The building still exists in Beacon Street. It appeared around 1861 listed to Joseph Gamble and was under the management of Mr and Mrs Albert Miles from 1890 to 1909 when it appears to have closed. The present use is for retail purposes; it was until the mid 1970s the Pheasant Café under the management of Mr & Mrs Mytton. The building stands opposite to the Little Barrow Hotel and is identified by the archway.

Beacon Street continued

21

Lemon Tree

Probably the prettiest name of any Lichfield pub, it still exists as a private residence numbered 125. It is listed in 1834, no doubt one of the new beer licences taken up following the Beer Act. In 1834 it is listed to Sarah Whitaker. In 1895 to around 1903 the landlord's name was **Fred Beer!** It then came under the management of Arthur Vernon Rockingham, the father of Fleetwood Rockingham who was landlord of one or two Lichfield pubs prior to the Second World War. It appears to have closed in 1915 under the last listed landlord Percy Woodfield, probably like so many pubs a victim of the war.

Feathers *

Still going strong although much altered during the last twenty years, the pub was listed in 1868-1892 as the **Prince of Wales Feathers;** the first listing of the pub is 1851 to a Robert Taylor. The photograph *right* was taken around 1914 on the occasion of the Sheriff's Ride as it returns to the City at the end of the day. The Feathers was at that time a very small pub, (you will see at the end of the row of cottages the sign for the Feathers) It expanded in later years to include all the cottages, which still are part of the present pub. The Mace Bearer at the head of the procession still carries out this function today and usually is on the verge of running as he reaches the top of Beacon Street as the horses gain a second wind and sense that home is near.

Fountain *

A pub still with us and much altered inside in the last twenty years, it appears around 1818 listed to Edward Collins. This part of Lichfield was in that period known as Newtown, a small but growing community that had sprung up at the junction of Beacon Street and what then was Grange Lane (renamed Wheel Lane later). The pub was rebuilt into its present exterior by the Lichfield City Brewery around the end of the 1916 period in what became known as *Brewery Tudor*. A splendid name of a landlord in 1880 is Jeremiah Craddock. The next-door foundry of Chamberlain & Hill had appeared by 1899 and the pub would have provided much needed thirst quenching for the foundry workers, the foundry finally being demolished for the supermarket, which now stands in its place.

Wheel/Catherine Wheel

The buildings in which this pub stood still exist and were for many years part of the offices to Tuke and Bell the other foundry that stood opposite the Fountain. The pub is listed in 1810 and was the site of an early tollhouse in the mid 1700s. At the rear of the **Wheel** stood the brewery of A.W. and W.A. Smith who had established their business in 1875. The Lichfield Brewery Co of St John Street who closed it and sold the premises in 1918 to Tuke and Bell, who manufactured parts for refuse vehicles and sewage equipment, acquired it. The site is now housing, but the premises of the **Wheel** still front Beacon Street along with their neighbours in the terrace. The road known as Wheel Lane was known as Grange Lane until around the turn of the century.

Beacon Street continued

Beehive

This pub, which stood on the right hand side of Beacon Street just past the entrance to the present day Wheel Lane, was first listed in 1848 as a beerhouse to John Nicholls. It had gone by 1911 and had reverted to a private residence as it is today. It is reputed to have had a sign with the saying *"Within this hive we're all alive, good liquor makes us funny, if you are dry then step inside and try the flavour of our Honey"*. How true this is, is anybody's guess, but it makes a good story.

Anchor

The photograph below shows the pub in the 1880s, which stood on the corner of what were Anchor Lane and New Road, later called Abnalls Lane and Beacon Street. The pub is first listed in 1834 to Thomas Baker, George Godwin held the licence from 1860 to 1890, and the pub was advertised for sale in the *Lichfield Mercury* in 1891 as "House for Sale".

It was demolished some years later and now forms part of gardens to private housing. To perhaps understand this part of Lichfield better you may wish to read Cuthbert Brown's books *"Born in a Cathedral City"* and *"Lichfield Remembered"*. Cuthbert Brown was born and raised here in Beacon Street and his books give a wonderful record of Lichfield between the wars.

1. Wheel   2. Beehive   3. Anchor   4. Present day site of Supermarket and former Foundry

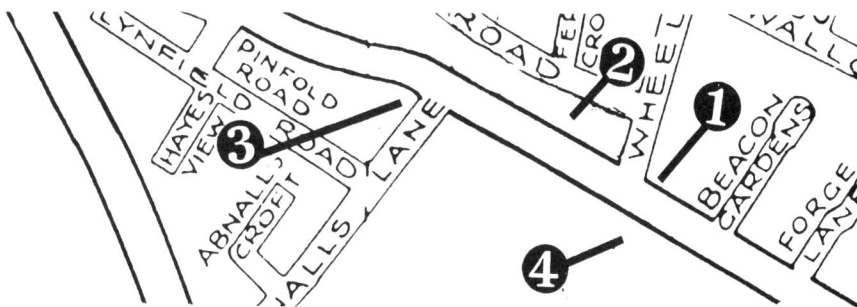

Note: Main map of Beacon Street appears on page 24

23

Beacon Street map

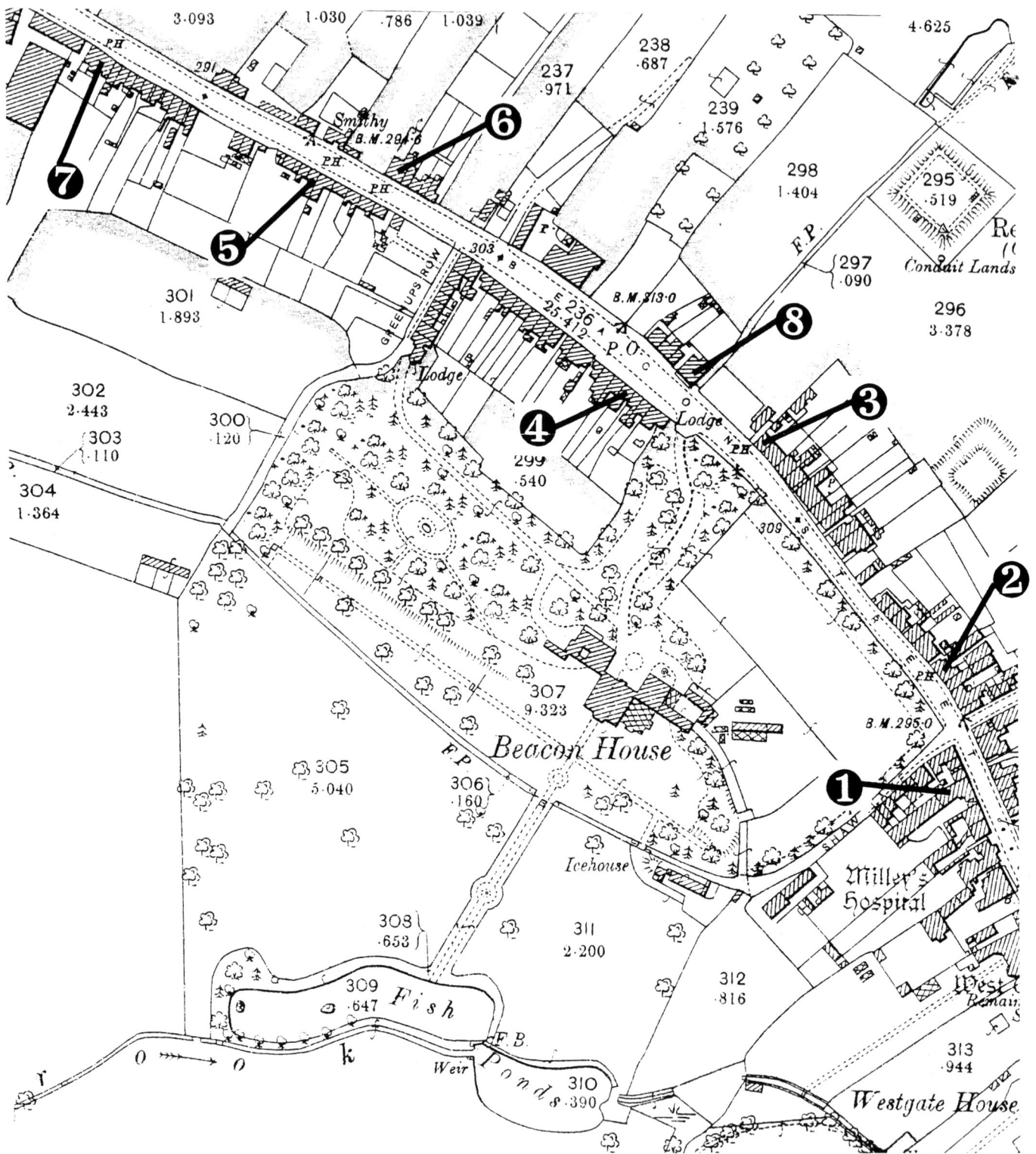

1. Coach & Horses   2.George & Dragon   3. Little George
4. The Pheasant   5. Lemon Tree   6. Feathers   7. Fountain
8. Present day Little Barrow Hotel for location purposes

24

The Earl of Lichfield *

Known locally as the **Drum**, the legend says that Recruiting Officers would stand outside to drum up recruits for the Army in the 1830s. The first listing is in the early 1800s to a Francis Middleton and named the **Mason's Arms**. It was purchased by the Anson family in 1842 and then re-named as the **Lichfield Arms,** the Anson family being the Earls of Lichfield, the pub's name in 1851. A very small one-roomed pub, the adjoining Barber's shop was taken in about 1970 and converted into a bar. The later re-ordering still shows the differing levels. The pub has on display some interesting photos showing the pub before this later re-building. Should it ever be re-named, then it ought to be named **The Drum**.

The photograph shows the pub in the period when the barbers shop occupied what later became the bar and the Central Garage with its swing-out over-the-pavement petrol pumps occupied the premises which is now McDonalds. It is also the period when the traffic flowed two-way along Conduit Street and the Market Place.

Malt Shovel

Now Dixon's store, it was converted into a shop in 1972, it closed as a pub in October 1971. The first listing is in an old deed dated 1592, used through the years by the market traders and the Waggoners who plied from here. In 1860 the landlord was the splendidly named Jeremiah Tricklebank who sold the pub in 1876 to the Lichfield Brewery Co. The census of 1841 lists not only the landlord, his wife, and a servant girl but also a resident Dancing Master.

The present building had the black/white mock Tudor effect during its latter years, it is now used as a store for an electrical retail outlet. The other two adjoining properties are still in existence and the archway along side the Bank is now used as an access to the car parks by Stowe pool.

Conduit Street and Dam Street continued

25

Windsor Castle

1818 sees the Windsor Castle listed to a Mr. Francis Eggington. It was probably used by the nearby stonemasons, Cathedral staff and the market day trade.

The present building No 16 Dam Street was a fairly plain fronted building as the photograph shows. The building now sports two Elizabethan looking windows on the first floor, these were fitted at the time of its conversion to a private house in the mid 1930s by Bridgemans the stonemasons.

In spite of it closing in the 1930s it is often forgotten by many old Lichfeldians when reminiscing. It did retain up to a few years ago its ramp in the cellar for the rolling of barrels.

The Englishman
Shown on St Mary's tithe map in 1848, it is now Tales Press and Art Shop. It is listed to Charlotte Grew in 1861 but had ceased to operate as a pub by the 1870s, no doubt reverting as many old pubs did to retail use.

It is thought to be the original building and the rear had the normal outhouses that were associated with early public houses; most pubs had buildings for brewing up to around the 1870s when the own brew fell out of favour and the large breweries came into their own.

Also listed in Dam Street:

Scott Arms
In 1834 the landlord is F. R. Wakelin, the premises being owned by the MP Sir Gregory Scott, the site has not been verified but known to be in Dam Street

Red Lion
Recorded in 1766 in Dam Street, but nothing is else known. Was the this forerunner of the **Windsor Castle** or the **Englishman?**

The Angel (now known as Samuel's) *

Listed by 1800, it was recorded that in 1828 a coach ran to Birmingham known as the Coburg, by 1834 this had become the Shepherd. A long-standing pub it did have some original decorated glass, the pub changed its name in 1978 to **Samuel's** to rebrand its image, still a popular pub with its clientele.

The Castle

The Castle is listed in 1793 to a David Cox and to his son John Cox from 1818 to 1850. Oxfam now occupy the premises, the lower frontage being rebuilt as a shop. The photograph shows the pub before its closure. A neighbour of mine recounts the day he moved into the Castle in 1933 when his father James Tonks became the new landlord: it was a rainy half-day closing day and they took the magnificent total of 5 shillings the whole day. The last landlord was William Norman Gallimore; the pub closing in 1963 and was converted to retail use the following year.

Scales *

A pub mentioned in the mid 1600s, it is listed to John Hill in 1793 and other members of the Hill family until 1834; the first Freemasons Lodge in Lichfield is recorded here in 1740. Known during the early part of the nineteenth century as the **Swan and Scales,** it was used as the weighing rooms for the races held in various parts of Lichfield before the development of the Lichfield course at Whittington Heath. The Scales had until its recent re-building some beautiful decorated windows containing the name. These were very much part of the pubs of yesteryear as they not only gave decoration but privacy to the customers. However the legislation of the day laid down that the lowest point of the engraving should not be more that 5 feet 9 inches from the pavement, enabling the local bobby to stand against the window and peer in to check for any unseemly behaviour, the minimum height for a policeman in those days being six feet. The windows during the re-development were sadly damaged and replaced with modern versions - enough said. The photograph shows the Scales in the 1930s.

Also listed in Market Street are:

Lion 1440

Eagle 1529

Nothing else is known of these.

27

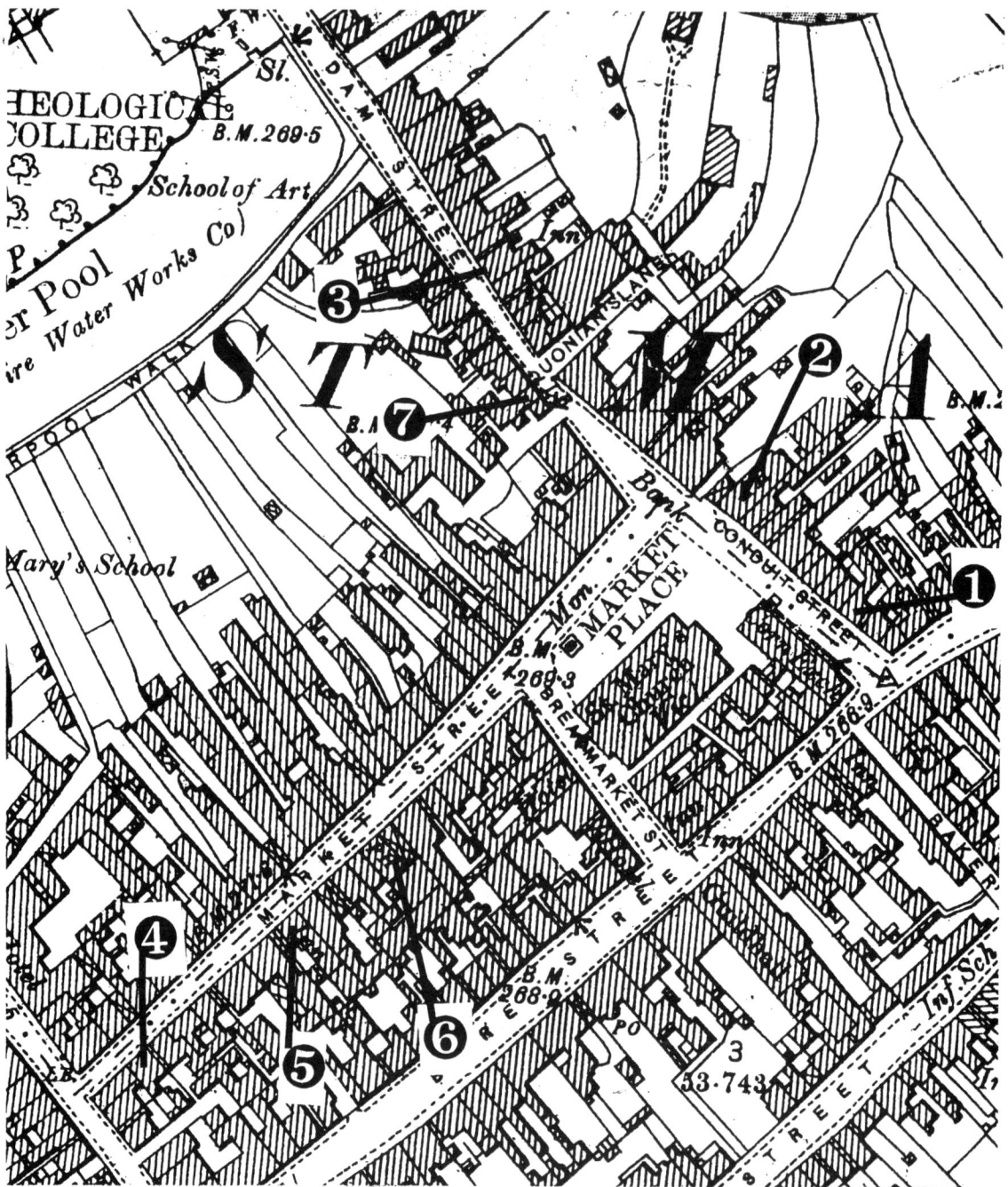

1. **Earl of Lichfield**   2. **Malt Shovel**   3. **Windsor Castle**

4. **The Angel**   5. **The Castle**   6.**Scales**   7. **The Englishman**

28

The Streets covered by this area are Church Street, Greenhill and Rotten Row; all these have been referred to loosely during the last hundred years as **Greenhill**. The Greenhill area is, along with the Cathedral, the oldest inhabited area of the City. In Norman times only the Cathedral and the Greenhill area existed, what we now call the City centre being a marshy and boggy area. The routes from the South and the East all joined here and there would have been an alehouse or two to provide food and shelter for travellers, who in that period would have been mainly pilgrims.

Greenhill as a large open area also had markets, a cattle market in the early 1800s until the building of the Smithfield market in the 1870s, and for many years during the period of Lichfield's major industry at the time, market gardening, was the meeting and loading point for the farmers to transfer produce onto the many carriers who would then carry the goods to markets in Birmingham, Walsall and the Black Country. The daily business of this trade of course required a large number of alehouses and Greenhill is rich with them, many of which have long gone or been long forgotten.

The main inns and alehouses which have been recorded have long and rich histories, the brief notes of each as follows are but a fraction of the history of this area.

The Smithfield

By the early 1800s a Smithfield market had been established on the site and by the late 1860s the Winterton family were established here, where they were to remain until 1988 and the move to Fradley. The Smithfield Hotel was built by the Lichfield Brewery Company in 1868 on land purchased from the Wintertons; the first recorded landlord was John Owen in 1868.

A very busy pub during the cattle sales and later auctions, it is remembered with some affection by Lichfield people, it being a centre of many community and voluntary organisations. It was built to serve the Smithfield Cattle market and on the removal of that market, lost its reason for existence. It has struggled on, changing its name for a period to **Three Spires** and even became a restaurant under the name of the **Sozzled Sausage** or something similar. At the time of writing it is being renovated into a Guest House or Hotel.

Blue Boar

Listed in 1830 to a John Burton, a member of a family that had a number of properties and licensed premises in the Greenhill area, it was run for some 25 years by William Gilbert. It is by the 1871 census named as the **Blue Pig**, and it appears to have closed by the 1881 census.

It stood on the site of the present entrance to the Greenhill Health Centre from Church Street. The buildings were used for other commercial and retail purposes until their demolition, and were used in their last days as a Café and Coffee Shop. St Michael's parish opened a workingmen's club here in 1878; in 1893 a Temperance society called the *Lighthouse Lodge of the Independent Order of Good Templars* was established here.

Greenhill continued

Curriers Arms

On St Michael's Tithe map of 1848, it is listed in 1861 to John Smith and served the many farmers and Waggoners who used Greenhill daily. It reverted to private housing in the late 1860s, it was known for a period as the **Carriers Arms,** (the business of a Currier, a leather worker, was a major industry at one time in Lichfield). The building still stands as many other buildings in this part of Greenhill, it is number 7 Church Street, next to the Dental Practice. A glimpse down the side passage through the iron gate will give you some idea of the timber framing of many of the buildings on Greenhill.

Spread Eagle

The building is still in use to-day as a Lock and Key shop. It is listed in 1834 to Thomas Thornloe a clockmaker, the family of Thornloe being the forerunners of the present day Jewellers shop of Salloway. 1851 to 1884 it is listed to John Thornloe, and remained in business as a pub until the late 1930s. The archway at the side is an indication of its previous use.

To be precise, although the Spread Eagle stands side-by-side with the Duke of York, the Spread Eagle is in Church Street, the Duke being officially in Greenhill as a postal address. Outside these premises what appears to be a narrow service road, is in fact the original A38 from Burton to Birmingham, the traffic before the new Bimingham Road in 1953, coming through here before descending Tamworth Street and then through Bore Street.

Duke of York *

One of Lichfield's oldest surviving pubs in both name and continued use of buildings. The Duke, as it is commonly known, is accommodated in a timber-framed building and has been extended in recent years by the inclusion of two neighbouring cottages. The name it is thought relates not to the *Duke of York of Ten Thousand Men,* but an earlier Duke of York who became James the Second. As the Duke of York he was a benefactor to the City, becoming James the Second in 1686. The pub first appears in Directories of 1818 listed to Johanna Dorrington but it had certainly existed long before that. It is not hard to imagine the kind of customers who would have thronged the pub when bull baiting was the major sport on Greenhill.

It was the principal pub when the Bower was the *Greenhill Bower;* it was decorated with hung meats in various forms, cooked on open spits or iron gates set over charcoal fires. If you imagine the horse traffic of the day and the piles of manure and dust with the inevitable flies it perhaps would not be too appetising. Harry Creswell who in the late 1930s was not only landlord but Lichfield's Chief Fire Officer ran the pub from 1915 to 1939. The pub is still going strong and has the feel of that old traditional country pub.

Greenhill continued

30

Bald Buck *

The modern Bald Buck was opened on the present site in 1957 to replace the original building, which was demolished to allow the Birmingham Road to be built . The original is first mentioned around 1810 but it had without doubt stood on that site somewhat earlier. In 1818 it is listed to Edward Maddox whose family ran the Bald Buck for over 50 years, the Maddox family being publicans in Lichfield for many years.

The above photograph gives a flavour of the old Greenhill, the buildings on the right hand side show the **Bald Buck** (the two-storey building) on its original site. The buildings on the left remain and the small cottages with the cart outside are still in retail use. One is David Fishers Butchers shop and the adjoining cottage is the building where in 1834 Daniel Proudman ran a small beerhouse called the **King William**. Behind the trees in the centre now stands the present Greenhill Medical Centre; just in the distance down Rotten Row stands the **Bluebell**. A great change from the present traffic chaos that now takes place in the rush hour.

Other pubs recorded through the years on Greenhill are as follows:

Fat Ox: Listed to James Burton in 1851, in one of the many cottages on Greenhill

Hole in the Wall: Site unknown, mentioned in Jackson's History of Lichfield of 1805

Jolly Gardeners: Listed in 1868 to George Burton probably the same pub as the Fat Ox of James Burton in 1851, St Mary's Tithe map shows a number of properties on Greenhill owned by the Burton family

Red Cow: Again mentioned in Jackson's History of Lichfield of 1805, nothing else known.

Greenhill continued

31

White Hart

Recorded in 1530 the White Hart stood on Greenhill until around 1810, the buildings it occupied are even older, recent surveys before their renovation into homes again following their closure for many years, show that this was an important Medieval Hall. After closure of the White Hart, it was converted into the poorhouse for St. Michaels in 1811 and remained as such until the new union workhouse was opened in 1840 in Trent Valley Road.

A sketch of the original building which illustrates the building as it would have been during the early life of the White Hart is as *right*. The blank parts are the area of the White Hart, the black and white gable was taken down and built with a continuous roofline up to the Duke of York as it is at present.

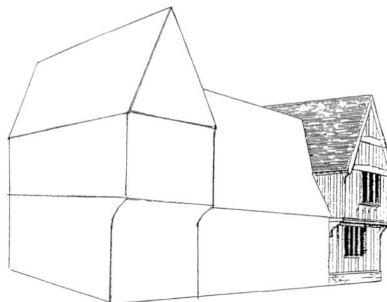

Bluebell

The Bluebell stood in Rotten Row, and since its closure in 1982 has been converted for use by a Housing Association. First listed in 1851 to George Alton, the last recorded tenants were Michael and Louise Walpole 1973 to 1981.

Wagon and Horses

A typical Greenhill pub with a name that suited the principal business in that area, it stood at the corner of Gresley Row- the site now a car park. The earliest recorded landlord in 1818 was a George Burton of the well-known Burton family. On the 1848 Tithe map of Greenhill it is listed to a member of that other well-known family of publicans, Edward Maddox. At that time the adjoining pub, the Bald Buck was being run by William Maddox.

The pub had gone by the late part of the Nineteenth century. The last recording I found is the 1871 census. The buildings were demolished along with its neighbours for the new Birmingham Road in the early 1950s.

Note: To fully understand the layout and sites of the Greenhill area and the pubs listed in this section a map appears on the following page which, hopefully, will explain the positions of these pubs in a clearer way.

Greenhill – Church Street – Rotten Row

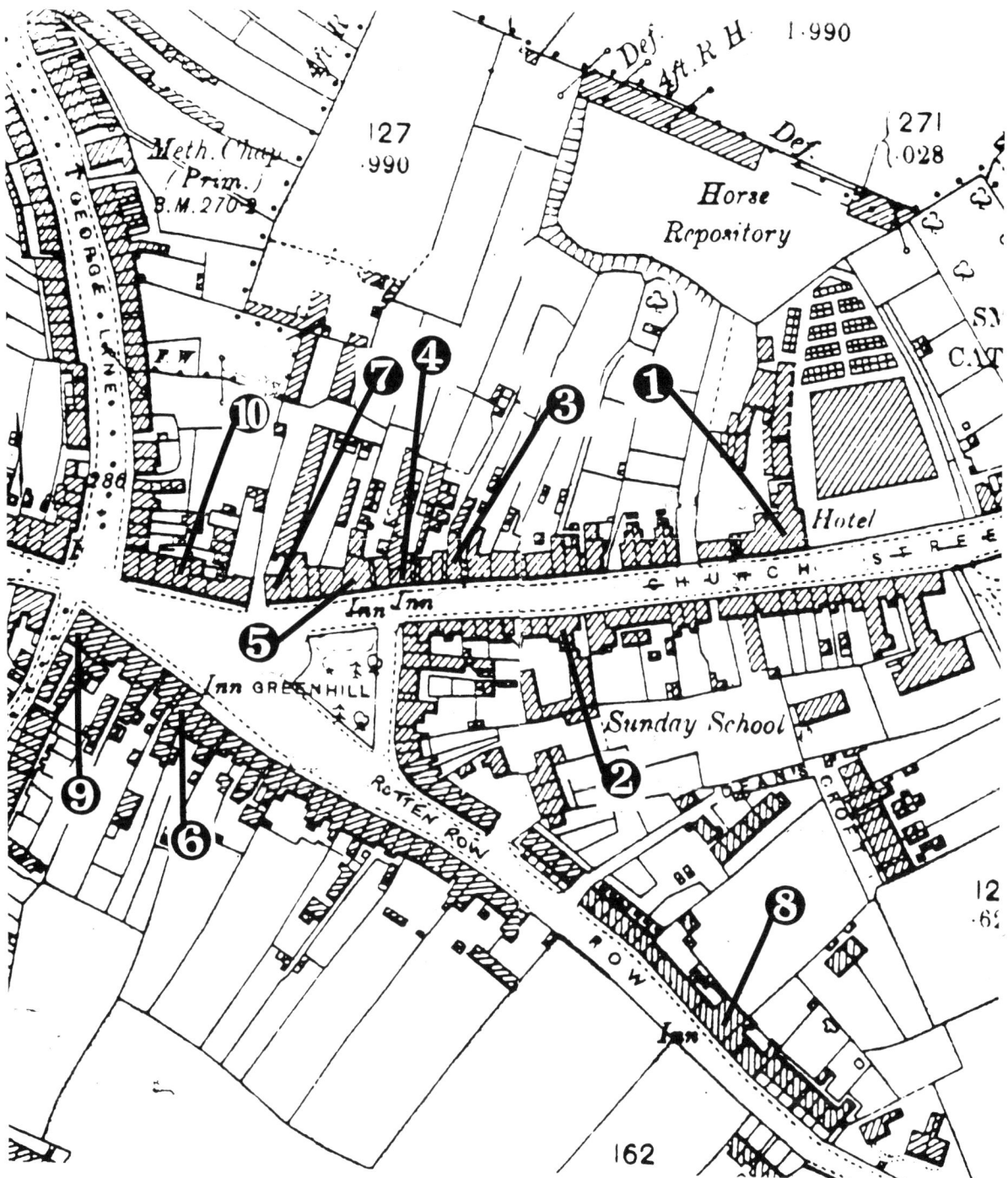

1. Smithfield   2. Blue Boar   3. Currier's Arms   4. Spread Eagle

5. Duke of York.   6. Bald Buck   7. White Hart   8.Bluebell

9. Wagon and Horses   10. King William

London Road

London Road was the principal route for coaches travelling from London to Chester and the North and was built on a causeway as far as the Tamworth Road junction as it crossed marshy ground.

Shoulder of Mutton *

The pub stood at the cross road of the London Road and the old Roman Road of Rykneild Street, which is now Cricket Lane, and Knowle Lane. This was for centuries an important junction for travellers and the many waggons which used Rykneild Street as a by-pass for Lichfield. The pub is listed in the 1700s. The name suggests that the original licensees were also Butchers; the field at the rear was in the early part of the nineteenth century used for pony racing. Deeds are in the Lichfield record office dated 1765. The pub still operates in its original function as a roadhouse serving food and drink to passing travellers.

White Lion

A small canal-side pub at the St John Street wharf; there were two wharves at this point as the canal, opened in 1797 crossed under the London Road. The pub is listed in 1818 to Rebecca Callow, in 1834 to 1861 a David Wood who is also listed as a coal dealer, the wharves having some 650 boats pass in a year in the mid 1800s, ran it. The pub closed as the traffic fell rapidly on the canal due to the arrival of the railways. The canal finally closing in 1954, it is thought the original building remained until the canal closure.

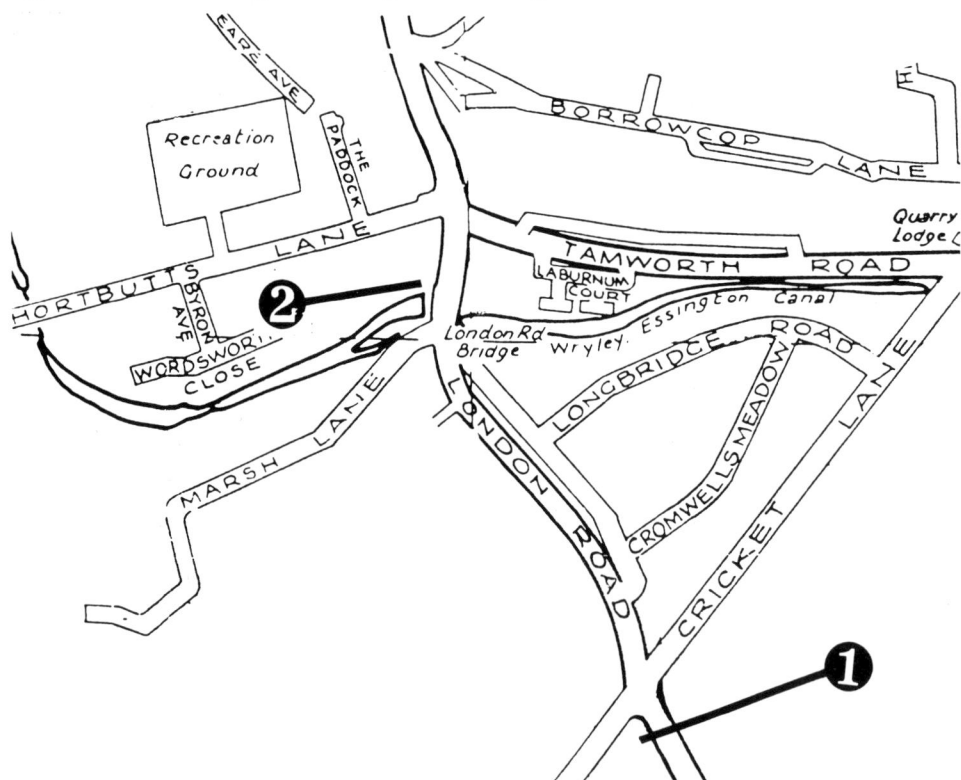

1. Shoulder of Mutton   2. White Lion.

Wade Street

Duke of Cambridge

The names of five pubs are listed through the years in Wade Street, which were found to be one and the same. In 1830 it is named **Fox and Hounds;** the **Tally Ho** from 1834 to 1851, 1860 shows it as the **Hare and Hounds,** and in 1868 it had become **The Cambridge,** finally taking its final name of **Duke of Cambridge** from 1880 to its closure or last listing in 1924, the last recorded landlord being Thomas Rowley. It stood on the left hand side of Wade Street going towards the Precinct and it finished its life as the offices to Clews the Builders. I was just too late to photograph it before its demolition. Houses now stand on the site.

Lord Rodney (Admiral Rodney)

Standing onto the frontage of Wade Street at the rear entrance to the Civic Hall it is listed in 1818 to one Thomas Garratt, the Garratts being Bakers in Lichfield for many years. Among the names of landlords are Spencer Shorthose and Tom Bowen; the last licensee, both of well-known Lichfield families. It was demolished with the clearance of the site for the new shopping precinct; the exact site is opposite the rear entrance to the Guildhall.

The view is of Wade Street, the building on the far right is the old Police Station replaced in the 1970s by the new building in Frog Lane. It was finally demolished being replaced by Home Lodge and shops. The road connecting Wade Street and Frog Lane, Castle Dyke, was opened with the demolition of the properties from the Police Station to approximately where the van stands in the picture. The Lord Rodney is sited just beyond the van.

The Precinct area continued

35

Bakers Lane

Levett Arms

The pub stood on the corner of Frog Lane and Bakers Lane. Bakers Lane is the line of the Precinct from Bore Street to the Birmingham Road but the whole of this area has changed so much, it would better to study the map of 1920 to understand the positions of the pubs in this group. Listed in 1834 to Edward Cork, the Levett Arms was still run by the Cork family in 1880. It was de-licensed in 1957 and sold for re-development.

The above two views show Quantrills Butchers shop, demolished to widen Bakers Lane for the new Precinct. The right hand view shows the view up Bakers lane and faintly in the distance is the Levett Arms beyond the cars. The left view shows the shop, which stood between Boots and the Old Crown now re-built as Dollond and Aitchison.

Gresley Row

Gresley Arms

Gresley Row still follows its original course but is now part of the road serving the car park and delivery entrance to the Precinct. The Gresley Arms stood on what is the delivery bay for the Argos store. In 1818 it is listed to Arthur Rowley and in 1928 to the splendidly named Fleetwood Rockingham; it closed in 1931, no known photographs exist. The main claim to fame is a fatal shooting at the pub in November 1878 when the landlord of the day a William George Green, loaded a gun with powder. By some mischance the gun had a marble in the barrel, and the gun went off killing a Walsall man called Samuel Bates drinking in the pub with two friends. The death was recorded as accidental death, the coroner expressing his misgivings at having to record this verdict. The inquest is reported in the *Lichfield Mercury of the 8th November 1878*.

Levetts Field

Railway Tavern

Originally known in 1851 as the **Bricklayers Arms** and licensed to William Smith whose family had a brick yard in the vicinity it had become the **Railway Tavern** in 1860 with a Thomas Smith as the landlord, probably the son of the earlier Smith. It was of course on the route from town to the City Station. In 1933/4 Mr Fleetwood Rockingham (see above) had taken over the licence. It closed with the building of the new Birmingham Road and the development of the land that now forms the Precinct.

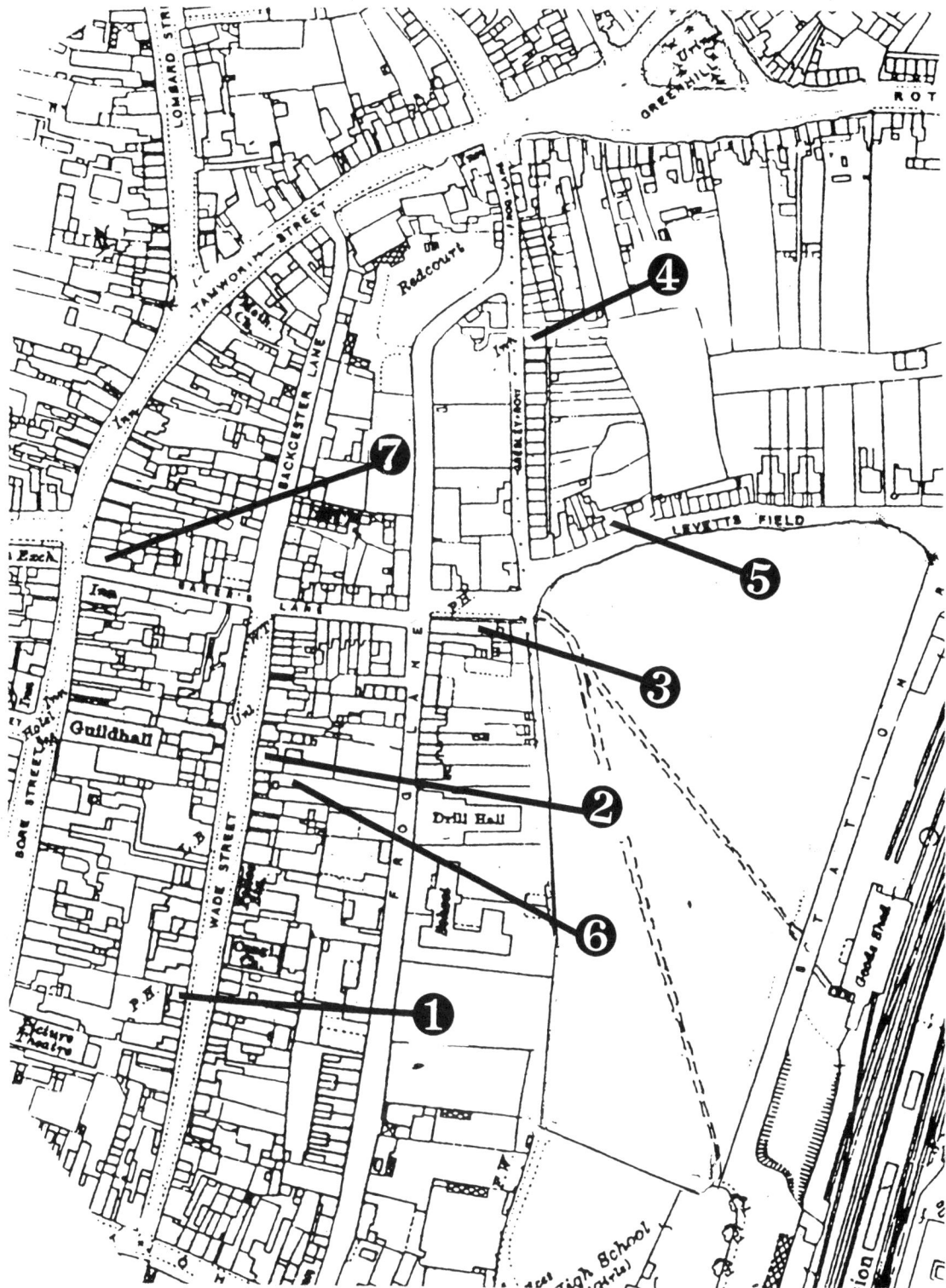

1. Duke of Cambridge 2. Lord Rodney 3. Levett Arms 4. Gresley Arms 5. Railway Tavern 6. site of Civic Hall 7. site of Quantrills shop

Constitution Inn

Standing as it did in a fairly isolated position did not affect the pub's trade. A popular venue and only closed due to the site being required for the new Western by-pass and traffic island at the junction with the Kings Bromley Road. The Constitution was first listed in 1868 to John Rushton; the exact site was on the opposite side of the then Stafford Road to the cottages, which still exist.

The last licensee was Gertrude Wood who is pictured in the splendid photograph below of the final night at the Constitution on the 8th June 1956. I am sure that this will bring back memories to many of the readers of this book.

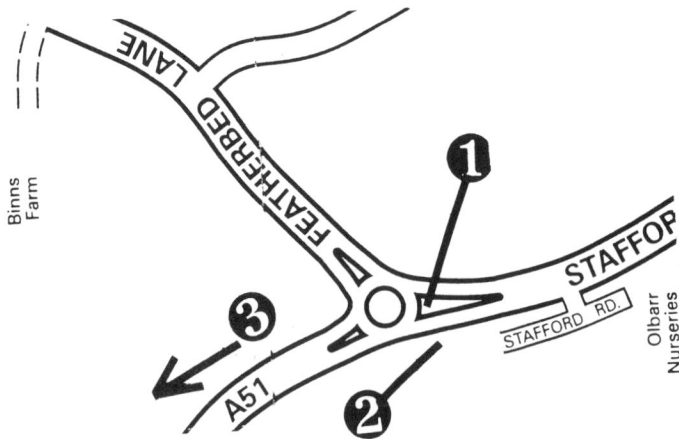

1. Constitution Inn   2. Existing Cottages   3. To Rugeley

Blueman

A beerhouse marked on St. Michael's Tithe map in 1848, it is listed to John Thacker. The pub had gone by 1862. It occupied premises in a row of houses opposite to Holy Cross Church. The area in the nineteenth century was known as *The Catholics*, the church of Holy Cross being built in 1803 before the Emancipation Act, many of its parishioners living close by.

Greyhound *

Listed in 1848 again on St. Michael's Tithe, its landlord being William Marklew whose family were brick makers in Lichfield at that time. It is still in existence to-day and still serving as a local pub. It had its own brewing facilities like so many pubs of the era.

City Arms

A Tavern in 1800 serving the coaching trade at that time, it is listed in 1848 to James Brooke. It had gone by 1862 no doubt due to the decline in coaching trade following the arrival of railways in Lichfield in 1849. It occupied premises, which were used for many years by Hiskins Garage. At the present time part of it serves as a hairdresser's.

Bridge Tavern

The pub is listed in 1862 to James Gething and from 1875 to 1892 it was under the management of his wife Anne Gething. It no doubt served the brewery workers from the Lichfield Brewery opposite and the trade from the coal drops and malt houses at the rear of the pub. The wonderful photograph shows the pub on Bower Day 1903 with the glorious array of customers and sitting regally in the centre (the only man without a hat!) is William Watkiss with his family. He was landlord from 1903 to the First World War.

St John Street continued

39

Lichfield Brewery

Brewing in Lichfield was a major industry and the Lichfield Brewery Co. offices still remain with the name over the door, although the Brewery buildings were demolished around 1969.

The Lichfield Brewery was formed by the amalgamation of two Lichfield breweries, those of the Griffith family and the Gilbert Bros in 1869. They built the new premises in St John Street in 1873. The Lichfield Brewery was taken over in 1930 by Samuel Allsopp & Co. who ceased brewing in Lichfield in 1931. The premises were used by the Lichfield Aerated Water Co. and then by Burrows & Sturgess who built a new works in Birmingham Road and as the Birmingham Chemical Co. produced essences and fruit juice compounds at the old Brewery. Who can forget the redolent air in the late 50s and early 60s? Burrows & Sturgess retained their upper St John Street offices and they became known as the Wiltell Works, the company's motto being *Quality will tell.*

Marquis of Anglesey (Anglesey Inn)

Built around 1817 it is named after Henry Paget, Earl of Uxbridge created the Marquis of Anglesey following the loss of a leg at the Battle of Waterloo as second-in-command to Wellington and becoming one of the nation's heroes. It was as this point that he was greeted by the Corporation and the Citizens of the City and feted following his return to Lichfield.

The last landlord noted is H. J. Wilson in 1939, the building becoming the Labour Exchange where so many young men joined the colours at the start of the Second World War.

The building was demolished to widen the entrance into the Birmingham Road, the pub's licence being transferred to the new premises in Curborough Road, the Anglesey Arms, in 1953.

Harts Horn

Lichfield's oldest known Inn, it stood adjacent to St John's Hospital just before the gates to the City and would have served travellers coming into the City. It is shown on Snape's map of the City dated 1780 and was probably a galleried Inn, and had gone by 1790. It stood on the site of the retirement home opposite Kennings.

Lord Nelson

The pub buildings still exist next to the District Council offices, which were the Masters house to the Grammar School. This is listed to Thomas Roberts in 1799 and by 1848 is marked on St. Mary's Tithe map to Joseph Higginson It was purchased by Chancellor Law, a benefactor to the City, presented to the Conduit Lands Trust who converted the premises, presenting them to the Grammar School for living accommodation. The building is still in use by the District Council.

St John Street continued

40

The Bear

It is first mentioned in 1698 and marked on maps of 1766. It stood opposite to the entrance to Throgmorton Street, now Frog Lane. It is recorded that it was served by Giles Tottingham's wagon to London, which took the remarkably fast time of 4 days, becoming known as the *Lichfield Flying Wagon*, roughly the time today to London using the M6 and M1! The Bear was demolished and replaced with the very fine town house, which still stands to day; it is used as a Private School.

Robin Hood

This pub existed in 1790; this long remembered hostelry has had a number of name changes during the last few years. The photograph shows the landlady in 1920, a Mrs Ada Madocks. The building was demolished in the 30s and rebuilt with a visibility splay to improve the view for drivers coming out of Frog Lane. The various name changes in the last few years were the **City Gate, City Frog** and **Funky Frog.** At the date of writing, October 2000, the second building we all probably remember is being demolished and replaced with housing. A splendidly named landlord was Ephraim Baldrick 1914 to 1918.

Red Lion

By 1810 the Red Lion occupied the corner of Wade Street and St John Street, at its final closure in the early 1930s it was demolished. The site is used for car parking, although neighbouring properties remain in use as offices etc.

In 1822-23 it is listed to Samuel Wayward and known then as the **Old Red Lion** which probably dates it well before 1810. Among the many landlords is Thomas Stringer of the famous Lichfield family and Miss Bessy listed from 1884 to 1904. The last licensee is Mrs Annie Statham 1924 to 1928.

41

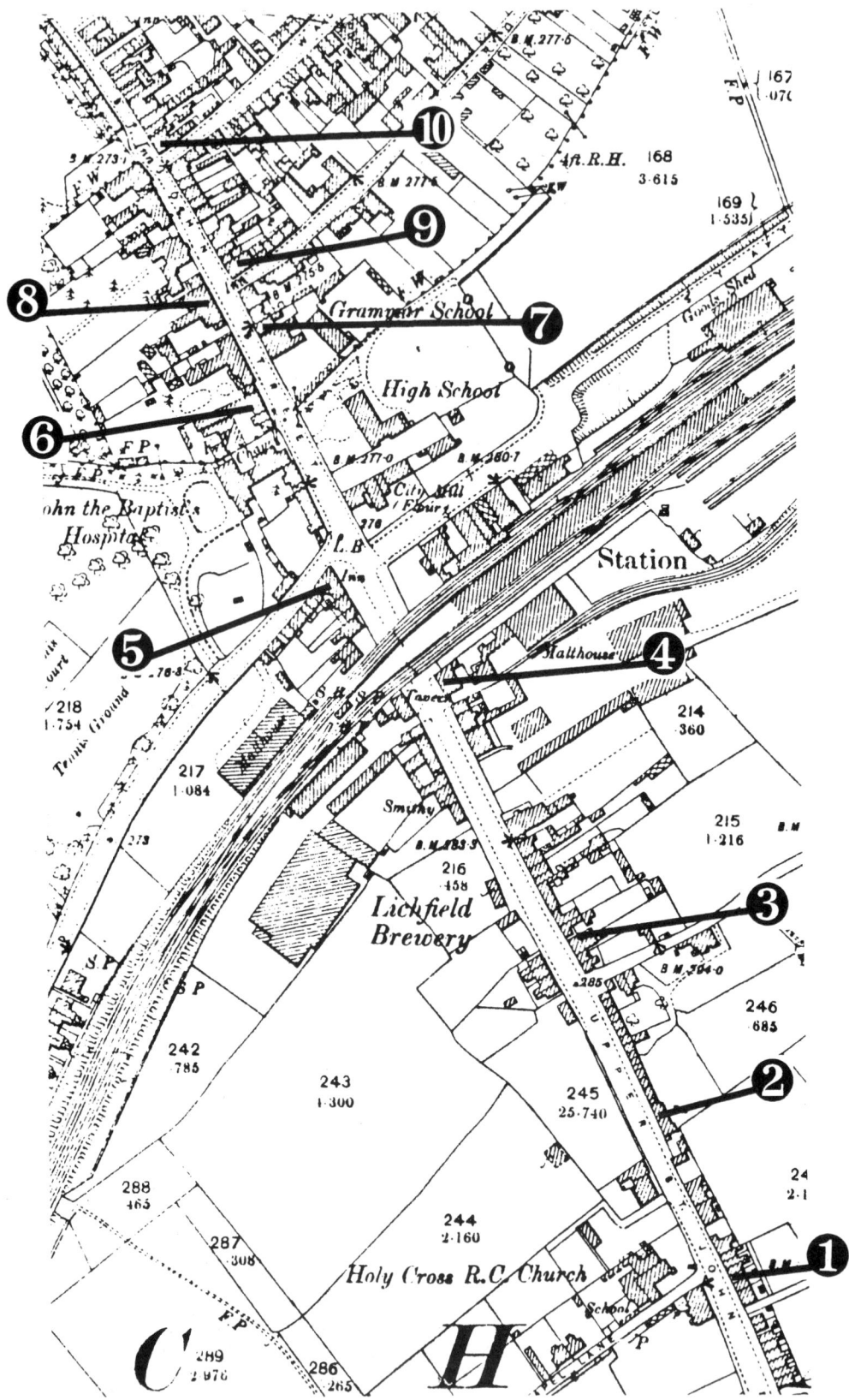

1.Blueman 2.Greyhound 3.City Arms 4.Bridge Tavern 5.Marquis of Anglesey

6.Harts Horn 7.Lord Nelson 8.Bear 9.Robin Hood 10.Red Lion

Horse and Jockey *

Marked on Snape's map of 1781, the Horse and Jockey still survives and offers a traditional pub atmosphere in the increasing tide of modernism in the city centre. The building is the original and is thought to be timber framed. The earliest recorded landlord is 1818 to 1841, a John Meacham.

Old Brewery

The premises are still in use to day and are used for offices. For some years from 1924 until the late 1970s Davenport's Brewery used the buildings as their distribution centre for the *'Beer at Home'* service in the Lichfield area. It was a brewery built by the Griffin Brothers at their second attempt following their original Brewery in Cathedral House, Beacon Street. The present premises were for years known as *The Old Brewery*, the photograph below shows the buildings with the Royal Oak next door circa 1910.

Royal Oak

One of two **Royal Oaks** in Lichfield not to be confused with the **Royal Oak** at Pipehill, although a landlord, James Worthington in 1875 was also a farmer and recorded in his will of 1872 as farming at Sandyway Farm which will be seen in the Walsall Road section as the original home of the **Royal Oak, Pipehill**. This pub in Sandford Street has existed since the mid 1700s, the earliest recorded landlord is Michael Berisford in 1793, the pub is shown on Snape's map of Lichfield dated 1781. It closed between the wars and the area is now used for car parking.

Sandford Street continued

43

Turks Head

Again this pub is marked on Snape's map of 1781. The name is one that stretches back to the long struggle of the Crusades. Standing as it did on the old route to Wolverhampton and Walsall before Queen Street was opened, it served the coaching trade. In 1828 it is the staging point of the *Umpire* between London and Liverpool alternating with the **Swan**. The earliest recorded name of a landlord is Thomas Slater in 1793. It was finally demolished to allow the extension of the Swan link road from Bird Street to the Friary as it stood across the new route; the colour slide taken in the 1980s on the front cover illustrates the pub in its final days.

The Tankard

This pub stood on the right hand side of Lower Sandford Street, being demolished for the new housing which now occupies the site. It existed in the late 1700s again serving the carriers following the old route to the Black Country towns. From 1818 to 1868 the landlord was Joseph Slater and from 1868 to 1877 Sarah Slater, some 60 years of one family running a pub, the Slater family being landlords of pubs in Lichfield over many years.

Hen and Chickens

The first listed landlord is James Nicholls in 1842. The pub stood at the top end of Lower Sandford Street on the left and had rear entrance from the new Queen Street and is a pub remembered by many Lichfield residents. The pub is listed in 1936 as 'licence not to be renewed. It reverted to a private dwelling house before being demolished to accommodate new housing.

Queen's Head * Queen Street

Errected in 1835, the first building in the *new* Queen Street built to straighten the road from the Walsall Road into Lichfield, they are called Queen Street and the Queen's Head as they were finally completed in the coronation year of Queen Victoria. The pub served for many years the community in that part of Lichfield and the nearby Gas Works and Foundry, Flowers Row and several more terraces, which had been built around that area from 1847. Sandford Street and Queen Street had by 1860 a fairly largish Irish community. The pub still continues and with the refurbishment of recent years has become one of the most popular of the traditional pubs in the City, a photograph taken in the early 60s on the front cover illustrates the pub in that era.

Also listed:

Paul Pry – Listed to E. Waldron in 1848, it appears from the St. Mary's Tithe that it was in the lower Sandford Street area near to the rear entrance to the Gas Works.

The Ship – 1818 to 1842 is the period this pub is listed. It is thought to be in the same area as the Paul Pry.

Blackboy – Listed in 1740 on the south side of Sandford Street in a lease in the Lichfield Records Office. Nothing else known

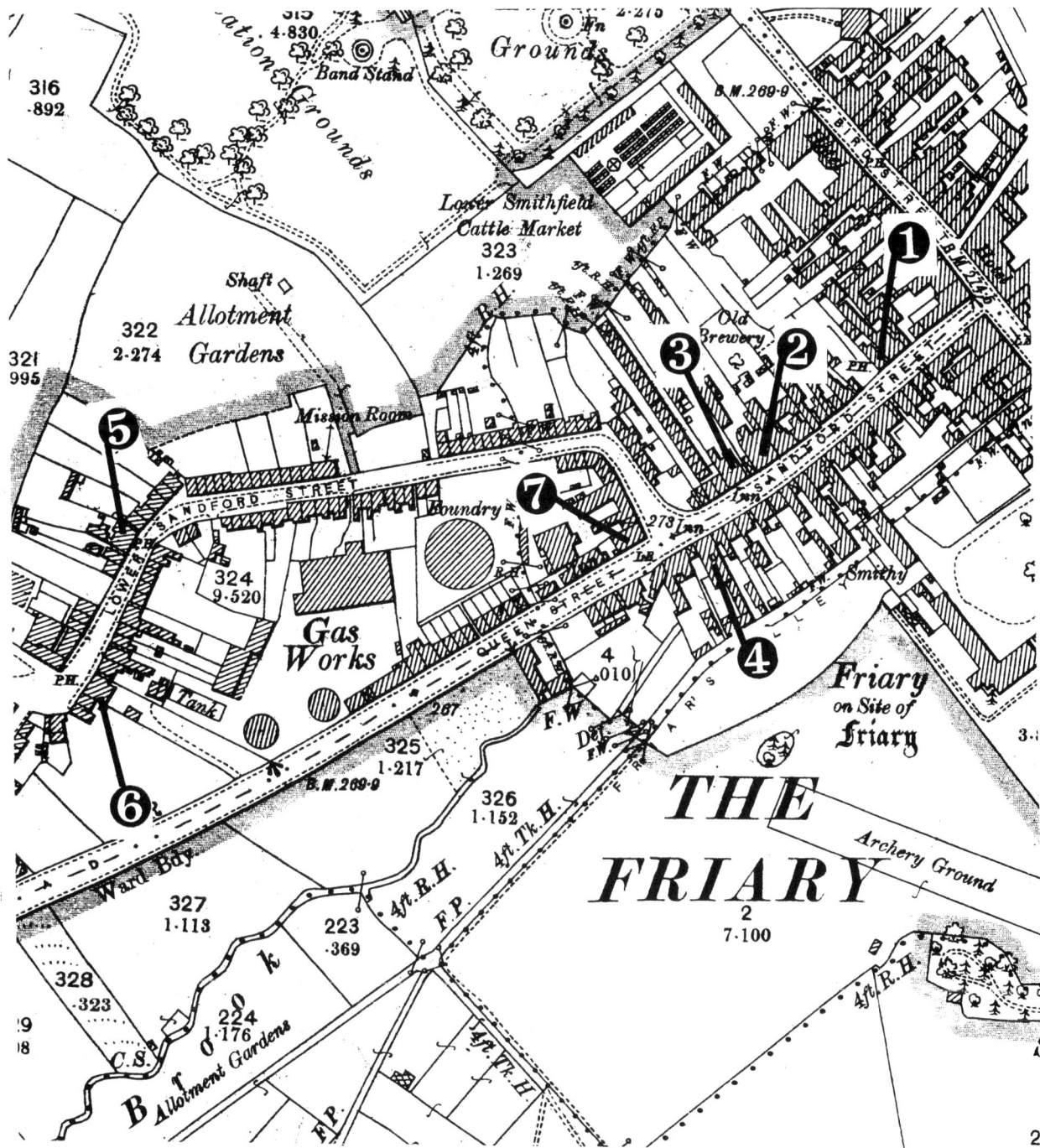

1. Horse & Jockey   2.Old Brewery   3. Royal Oak   4.Turks Head

5. Tankard   6. Hen & Chickens   7.Queens Head

"Oh mortal man that lives by bread
What is it that makes thy nose so red?
Thou silly fool, that looks't so pale
'Tis drinking Sally Birkett's ale."

Chequers

The Chequers was demolished in 1970 when the whole of Stowe Street was re-developed. The pub is first listed in the late 1700s and was always the centre of entertainment in this part of Lichfield. It stood on what is now the traffic island at the Stowe Pool end of Stowe Road. The last listed landlady is Mrs Edna Lyons. The Chequers is remembered with great affection by the residents of the old Stowe Street.

Seven Stars

Listed in 1771 it was along with the Chequers on the original route from Lichfield to the North before the widening of the Bird Street bridge. It stood opposite to what is now Partridge Croft, being demolished along with its neighbours at the re-development. It can be seen in the photograph of Stowe Street taken around 1960; if you stand by the shops and look towards St Chad's you will see the total change to the street.

Ring of Bells (or Eight Bells)

A genuine old Public House opened in a private dwelling, it is listed in 1834 to Thomas Walton who was also the Sexton and Clerk at St Mary's, he claimed to have known " the Great Doctor" when working as a boy for old Michael Johnson. It is said that Thomas Walton often adopted airs and imitated the Doctor, even correcting his customers' grammar and pronunciation.

The photograph is taken about 1910. It shows the landlord of its time looking for customers. He is W. Slater and was known to all as *Ava Slater*, he was re-owned for his *"go on ava nother one"*.

Stowe Street continued

Britannia Inn

Listed in 1818 to Thomas Salt, it stood on the same side of the street as the Seven Stars; the site of the Britannia is the forecourt to the present shops. This is probably appropriate as the Pub was de-licensed in 1927 and converted into a general grocery.

Alice Baker was the licensee of the Britannia from 1912, followed by her son from 1914 to 1916. Alice had previously kept the **Dog and Partridge** since 1911, having taken over from her husband who had been there since 1861. This makes a total of 55 years of one family running pubs in Stowe Street.

Staffordshire Knot

Thomas Foster is listed as the landlord in 1861. This was a beer only house until March 1960 when it obtained a Full Licence. It was at No. 55, a popular pub with many residents of Stowe Street up to its closure.

Dog and Partridge

No. 48 opposite to the Staffordshire Knot, this was a Beerhouse in 1861 listed to Thomas Barker and managed by his wife Alice Barker in 1911. The pub closed before the First World War.

Cross Keys (Lombard Street)

The Cross Keys stood alongside the entrance to the car park next to the WI Hall, now rebuilt as a Jehovah's Witness hall.

The photograph is dated 1970 just before it was demolished for the present housing scheme. The Cross Keys are listed to James Gee in 1834. The pub was run by members of the Ffrench family from 1914 to 1955, a total of some 41 years.

Also Listed:

The Boot (Stowe Street) Listed as a Beerhouse in 1834, it stood at the entrance to the Albion Mills.

The Volunteer (Lombard Street) It is mentioned as being kept by Elizabeth Shaw from 1816 to 1822. There is no record later than that date. The members of the Lichfield Volunteers, the Home Guard of its day, probably used it. Its site has at present not been verified.

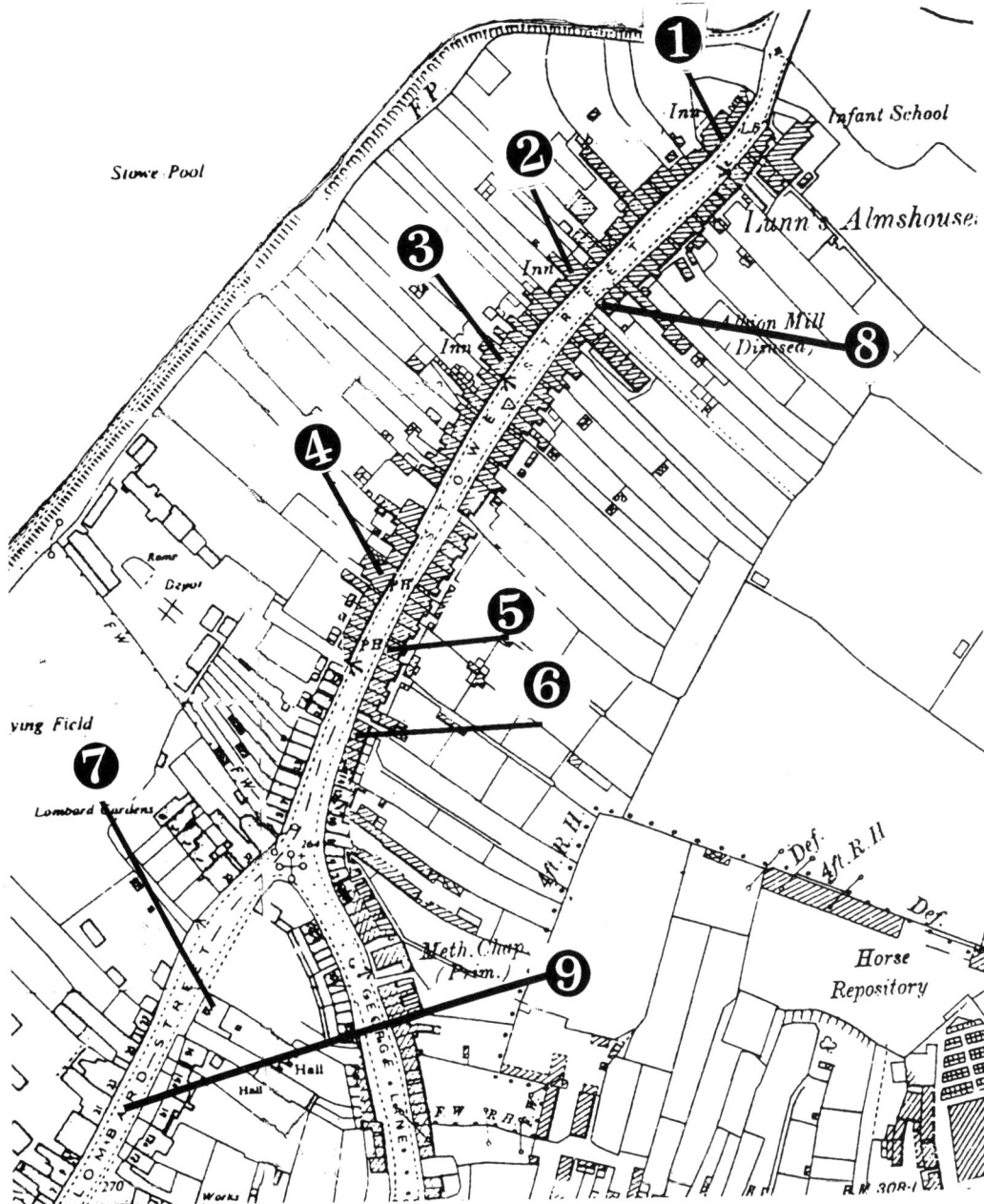

1. The Chequers   2. Seven Stars   3. Britannia   4.Staffordshire Knot

5. Dog and Partridge   6.Ring of Bells   7. Cross Keys (Lombard Street)

8. The Boot   9. Volunteer (Lombard Street)

Within this hive we're all alive
Good liquor makes us funny,
If you are dry step in and try
the flavour of our honey.

Sign often seen over Taverns called The Beehive

Trent Valley and Old Burton Road

Railway Inn

This was the first Railway Inn in Lichfield, not to be confused with the pub of the same name in Levetts Field. It opened in a Farm House known as Bexmore Farm and stood across what is now the start of Eastern Avenue. It was to serve the new railway station of the Trent Valley line from Stafford to Rugby. The landlord at its opening was the farm owner Francis Sharrod; the pub at that time was officially in the parish of Streethay it only coming into the City area in the 1930s. The Trent Valley Station of that time stood on the other side of Trent Valley Road at the rear of what is now the Trent Valley Hotel. On the opening of the *new* Trent Valley Station on its present site the **Railway Inn** had some competition as the present **Trent Valley Hotel** was opened in 1877. It closed and Francis Sharrod became the first landlord of the new pub. It reverted to farming use and was finally demolished on the opening of the new Eastern Avenue and the Industrial Estate.

Trent Valley Hotel *

Opened as set out above in 1877 on the opening of the *new* Trent Valley Joint Station, it was to provide not only accommodation for rail travellers but food and drink whilst they awaited their trains; as many present day rail travellers from Trent Valley will tell you, we could do with it today. The horse bus between the City Centre and Trent Valley ran from here. It was also a busy pub for the many farmers from the Alrewas and Burton areas, travelling into Lichfield on a daily basis with their market garden produce, to call and no doubt have a drink to help them on their way.

Trent Valley Brewery

One of Lichfield's Breweries, it stood on the Streethay side of the Trent Valley Station with rail access from both the Low and High level lines. It was built in 1875 amalgamating with the Lichfield Brewery of St John Street in 1891. It was finally demolished in 1970 and it is now a Car Rental storage area.

Yew Tree – Old Burton Road

Listed in 1834 to a William Sharrod of the same family that ran both the Railway Inn and the Trent Valley Hotel, it had gone by the 1870s. It served the traffic and trade passing along the Burton Old Road before the present Trent Valley Road was built in 1840. It would have also served the original station on the Burton to Walsall line, which stood east of the present rail crossing in Old Burton Road; the footpath to the Trent Valley still exists. The joining of the two rail lines into the London North Western Railway and the building of the joint station on its present site helped to take away the pub's reason for existence. The buildings still remain and are called Yew Tree House.

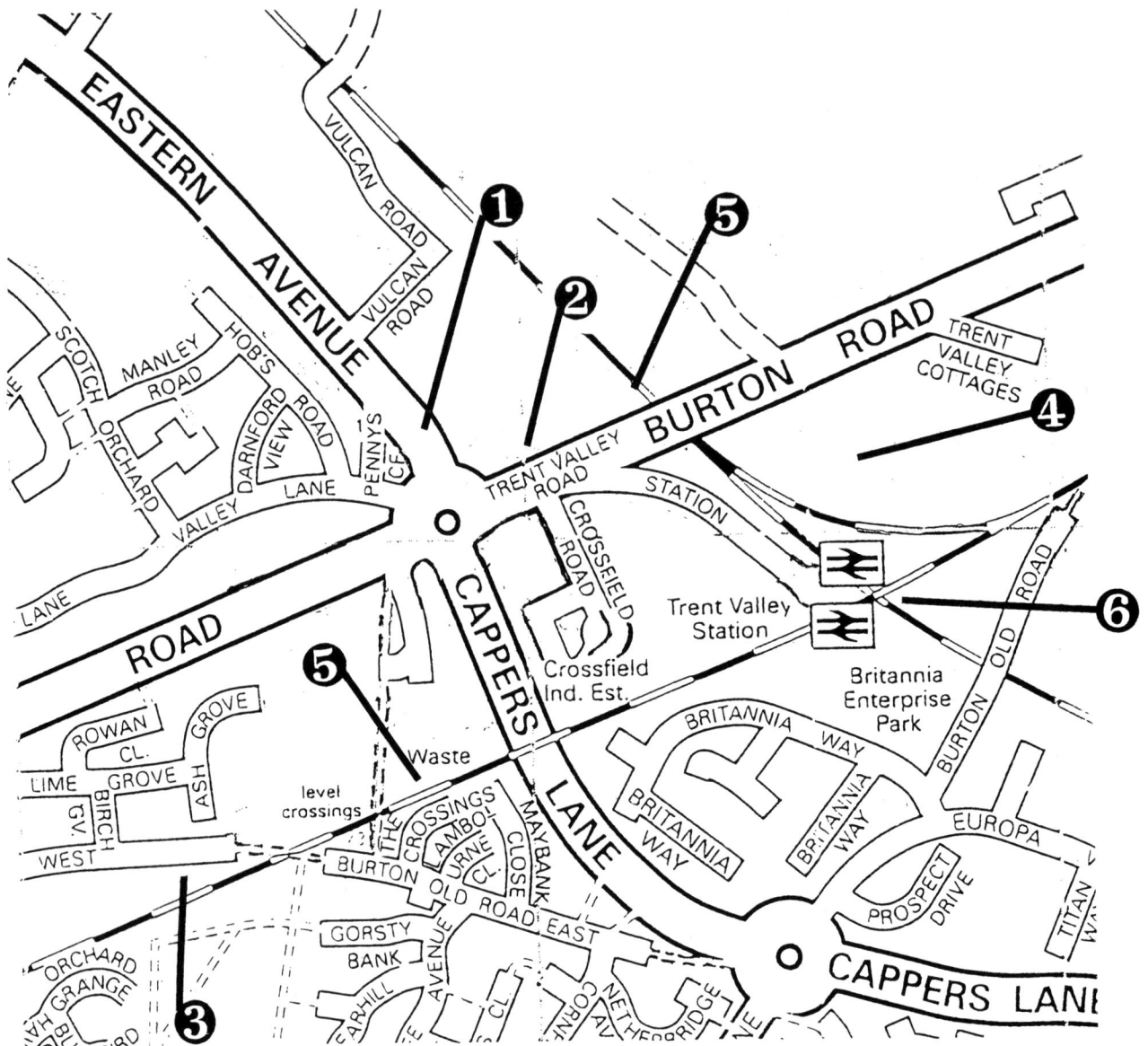

1. Railway Inn   2. Trent Valley Hotel   3. Yew Tree Inn

4. Trent Valley Brewery   5. Site of original Trent Valley Stations

6. Present Trent Valley joint Station

Carpenter's Arms * - Christchurch Lane

This pub has the typical history of so many pubs in the country; it is recorded on the tithe maps in 1848 as a house and garden somewhat isolated from other properties in the area, and it is listed to James Page. By 1851 James Page is listed as a *Carpenter and Beerhouse keeper;* by 1860 the beerhouse is being run by his wife Martha Page who is listed as a *Beerhouse and Beer retailer,* which description indicates an *On* and *Off* licence and by 1880 the pub is finally recorded as **The Carpenter's Arms.** This pubs history illustrates how so many un-named beer retailers' outlets became Public Houses and thankfully this one is still serving its local community.

Black Horse – Walsall Road

A short-lived pub, the building still stands on the Walsall Road. The house was built in 1832, by 1851 it is listed to William Waldron, by 1861 William Waldron is listed as a Cattle Dealer, no mention of the Black Horse. This was a short lived beerhouse opened probably to serve the passing waggon trade of the market gardeners on their way to Walsall with their produce. Walsall Road up to Pipehill is a steep climb and the Black Horse would have provided trace horses to waggoners to assist up to the top. This trade would have also been carried on by the other pubs on the Walsall Road, then known as "Sandaway". The building is the first house past the new roundabout and houses, which are being built at the time of writing.

Royal Oak –(Sandaway) – Walsall Road

This still existing House on the opposite side of the Road to the **Three Tuns,** is recorded in 1811 to George Holdcroft and is called the Royal Oak. Again its purpose was to serve the waggoners and provide trace horses for the climb. By 1818 it is listed to a J.Sadler who held the pub until 1860 when it was taken over by Henry Litherland. The pub appears to have closed around 1868, moved up the road and relocated into the premises that are remembered by many as the **Royal Oak.** The Sandaway buildings then became a farmhouse again and remained as such until a few years ago when it suffered a fire. At the time of writing it still remains semi-derelict.

Three Tuns * - Walsall Road

This pub, still existing, is first recorded as such in 1771; the name is the sign of the *Company of Vintners,* a tun being a barrel containing 252 gallons. The pub would have served the waggon trade, a roadhouse of its day and it still serves the modern trade. A memorable name of the many landlords is one Jethro Scoffham in 1860.

Walsall Road continued

The Royal Oak - Pipehill

Moved up the road in 1868 and first listed to Charles Small, this is one pub many people remember but cannot remember its name. The picture illustrates it in the 1960s; the only remaining sign is the little lay-by on the left of the road just before the top of Pipehill. The **Royal Oak** was one of the last beer-only houses in the City, the last recorded landlord was Harry Wright. The pub closed in the mid 1960s and the buildings were demolished in 1968. To look at the site it is difficult to believe that a pub stood here. Most of the rubble remained on the site, which is now overgrown giving little sign of its existence.

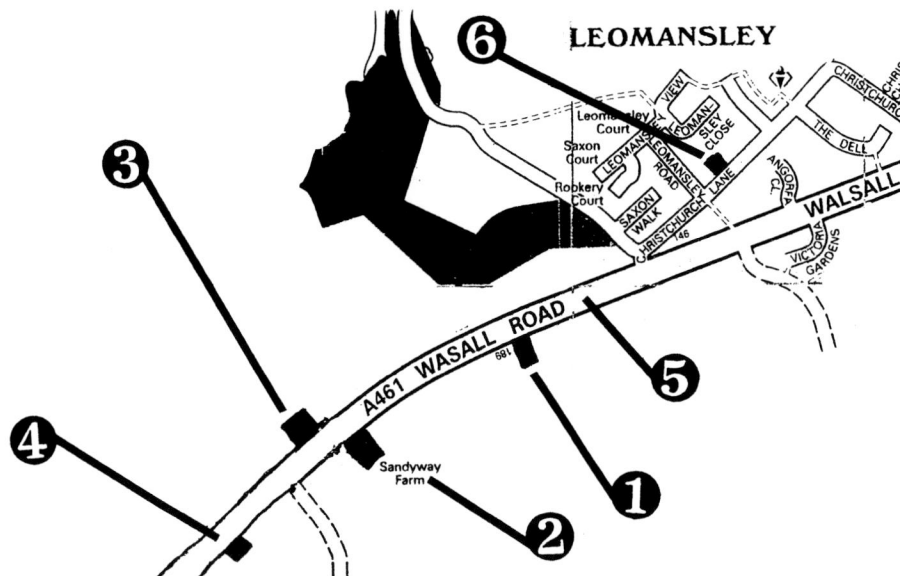

1. Black Horse   2. Royal Oak, (now Sandaway Farmhouse)

3. Three Tuns   4. Royal Oak – Pipehill   5.New traffic island

6. Carpenter's Arms (Christchurch Lane)

Bull's Head

Now the Greenhill chip shop, the pub is listed in 1810 to Phillip Salt. Little is known of this pub other than it finally closed in 1910/11. The last known landlord was an Octavos Wright. It is still the original building and stood sentinel with the Holly Bush guarding the entrance to the City at the Tamworth Street Gate.

Holly Bush

This pub with its opposite number is again listed in the early 1800s. In 1818 it was run by a William Maddox, a family that figures often in the Lichfield pub trade - see the Robin Hood for another member of this family. It was rebuilt into the present form in 1878 giving it a classical pub shape. It had a second name **Knights** for a short period in the early 1980s and converted into a Chinese restaurant as it is to-day. Little alteration was carried out to the façade other than that the corner entrance was sealed off. A photograph taken in 1960 in colour appears on the front cover that gives an excellent guide to how the pub appeared to countless people over the last 100 years.

Golden Ball

It appears in 1842 listed to Charles Stringer who moved here lock stock and barrels together with the name from what became the George the Fourth in Bore Street. It is listed also as **The Ball,** and appears on St Mary's Tithe map of 1848 as the **Old Golden Ball.** The pub changes its name once again in 1901 when it is listed as the **Saddler's Arms** to an Elizabeth Starkey. It is now the Dolls House shop.

King's Arms

This is listed in the late 1700s. The entire frontage was rebuilt as shops in the 60s but the rear buildings accessed from Lombard Street remain and are used as a Mexican Restaurant at the time of writing. The pub had gone by 1900; the last known landlord is C. Slater in 1899. Among the names of landlords through its life are Stringer, Gee and Sherratt, names that appear on a regular basis in Lichfield pubs. The present frontage consists of shops, among them a sewing machine shop.

Coachmaker's Arms

A short-lived beerhouse standing next to the Methodist Church, it is now a Restaurant and is in the original building. In 1828 and 1834 it is listed to John Heap. The Heap family at that time were coachmakers in St John Street. By the Tithe map of 1848 the pub had gone and is listed as a private dwelling house to a William Heap. The name obviously related to the family business.

Tamworth Street continued

The Grapes

Little is known about this pub. In 1893/9 it is listed to John Abdellah as a Hairdresser and Beer Retailer. It is mentioned in the Lichfield Mercury of 24th November 1899 as being for sale by Auction. It occupied the corner premises alongside the old Regal cinema, the top storey being removed some years ago, and is currently used as a clothes shop 'Country Casuals'.

The Mitre

Now used as an amusement arcade, the Mitre is listed in 1818 to Nicholas Virrells. The last listed landlord is Tom Bowdler in 1911; it appears to have closed around 1912/13. The building is little changed on the upper floors façade, the ground floor being changed through the years to suit the various retailers that have used the building.

The Acorn (Pig and Truffle) *

The Acorn, not to be confused with the *newly* named **Acorn** next door; the old Acorn's name is now **Pig and Truffle**. The pub has been on the present site over two hundred years; the frontage was rebuilt in the mixture of *Brewery Jacobean* some years ago. The pub was sadly renamed in 1988. The pub was in the Hine family's hands from 1958 to 1973 under Les Hine, and then his nephew Chris Hine from 1973 to 1985.

Also listed:

Old Crown

Not to be confused with the **Old Crown** in Bore Street, this pub is shown on Snape's map *(below)* of 1781 marked No **1** opposite to what is now Boots Chemists and towards the corner with Conduit Street. The second **Old Crown** is shown on the same map in Bore Street marked No **2**. The Old Crown listed in Tamworth Street is mentioned in Parker's history of Lichfield as being the home of a Masonic Lodge in 1784, describing the property as being situated at the corner of Tamworth Street and Conduit Street (formerly Butchers Row).

Little else is known about this **Old Crown** in Tamworth Street. It appears to have gone by the early 1800s. Was this an annexe to the **Old Crown** in Bore Street?

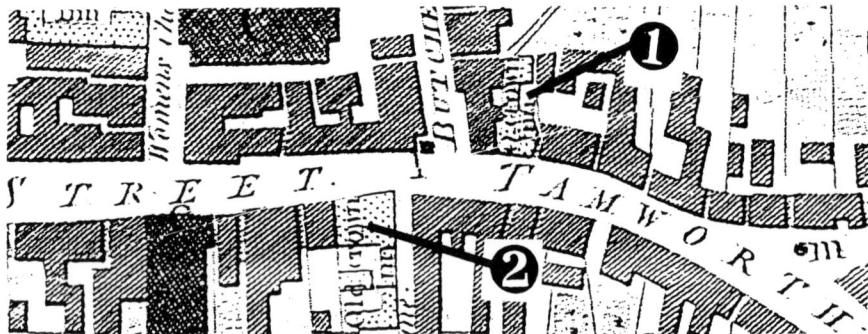

Tamworth Street

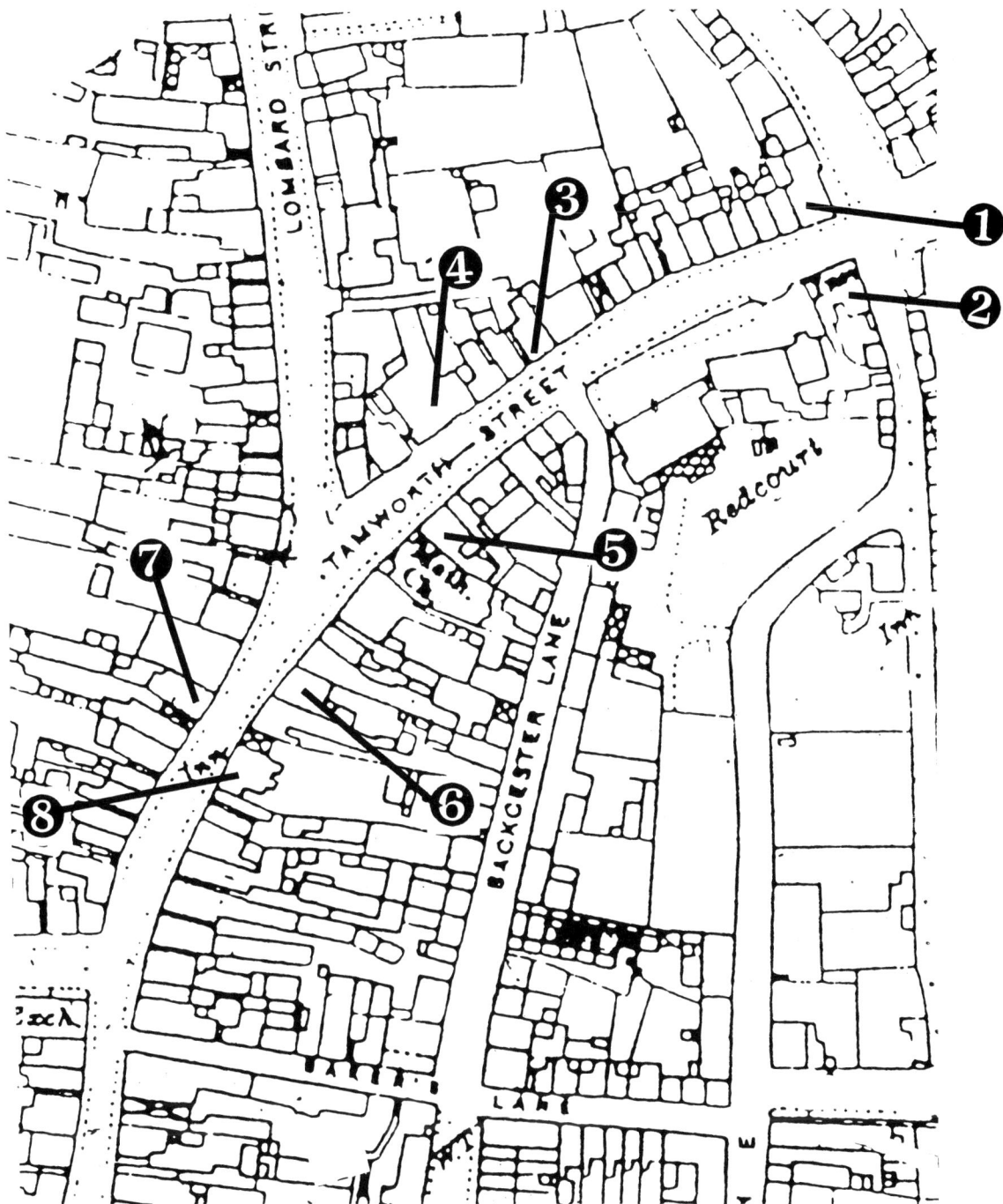

1. Bull's Head   2. Holly Bush   3. Golden Ball   4. King's Arms

5. Coachmaker's Arms   6. The Mitre   7. The Grapes

8. The Acorn

Inn Signs and their meanings

Inn signs and their names could be the subject for a book in its own right. The practice of erecting Inn Signs first appears in the Roman period; the Roman sign for a tavern was a bush of vine leaves, hence the saying 'a good wine needs no bush'. Anglo-Saxons identified their Taverns by a pole decked in evergreen. After 1390 it became compulsory for innkeepers to display a sign or "Alestake" - at a time of mass illiteracy it was the only way of proclaiming one's trade.

The origin of names of inns and taverns is obscure. Many refer to various historical events, trades, royalty and religious symbols; animals, heraldic objects and local landowners were also popular. Lichfield pubs were rich in all these areas. Some names are quite clear, for example, Duke of Wellington or Lord Nelson, both national heroes; however listed below are some with names that have sometimes one or two meanings

ADMIRAL RODNEY/LORD RODNEY   A seafaring hero. Listed in 1848's tithe map as Admiral, it changed in later years when he was elevated to a peerage.

ANCHOR   Originally a religious name but for pubs on inland sites without any connection with canals, usually referred to a former sailor settling down to a new life.

ANGEL   An early religious sign usually found in Cathedral Cities, it originally referred to the Annunciation of the Blessed Virgin.

ANGLESEY ARMS/ MARQUIS OF ANGLESEY   Local landowners and hero of the Battle of Waterloo.

BEEHIVE   The only sign referring to an insect, it often indicated the innkeeper,s second trade and had a sign with an amusing rhyme.

BOARD   A very popular sign some hundred and fifty years ago. The name of course refers to the "*Board*" or table upon which were set the cold joints, pies and game. Later on it became customary to place these on the *Side*board, from this term we obtain the words "Sideboard", "Boarding House" or "Board and Lodgings".

BRIDGE   Refers to the railway bridge over St John Street, a highly decorative bridge and a popular tourist attraction in its early days.

CHEQUERS   Name obtained from the practice of painting the posts of signs in alternating black and white. It is also a sign that appears in many coats of arms of some local families. Once a very popular sign, now very few remain.

COACHMAKER'S ARMS   This name can also include **Currier's Arms** and **Saddler's Arms** as this name relates to the trade that the landlord often had worked in or his second trade. It also was a way of tradesmen of a particular trade gathering together without them contravening the law when the Combination Act was in force.

CONSTITUTION   This name often given to pubs, which were close to urban areas but required a walk in the countryside to reach them, fine in good weather. No doubt a cycle was useful when time was called.

CROSS KEYS   The symbol of St Peter, an old sign with roots back in early Christian times, also part of the Papal arms.

DOG & PARTRIDGE   This sign of which there are many variations, was originally intended to advertise the fact that game was sold at the house either before or after the acquisition of a licence to sell wine and beer.

DUKE OF CAMBRIDGE   Grandson of George III, he was Commander-in-Chief of the British Army until the 1890s and a major opponent of military reform. His resignation was insisted upon by the House of Commons at the age of 76.

FEATHERS   The meaning is the Fleur de Lys and the badge of the Prince of Wales

FOUNTAIN   Popular in medieval times.   Associated with the martyrdom of Saint Peter.

GRESLEY ARMS   This name (similarly **Levett Arms, Lichfield Arms, Scott Arms** and **Anglesey Arms**) relates to local landholders.

HOLE-IN-THE-WALL   The name is taken from three different causes, (a) a hole in the wall of a condemned cell through which a prisoner was allowed to speak before execution, (b) a hole in a debtors' prison in which better food was passed, of course on payment, and heavy at that, (c) a hole in a leper's den through which certain brave souls of the church would thrust their hands to bless the dying men and women.

KING'S HEAD   Also the King's Arms. The sign never said which King.   The Monarch could change quickly in those uncertain times.

LAMB   Always found in Cathedral Cities, the sign would have been the Pascal Lamb (Agnus Dei) and popular before the reformation. Inns of this name would have been close to the Cathedral and often owned by them.

PAUL PRY   Named after the character in John Poole's comedy "Paul Pry" which was played in 1825 and refers to a man who has no occupation of his own, and is always meddling in others people's business

RING OF BELLS   Also includes the **Eight Bells** and so called because the landlord was also the bell ringer at a Church with a peal of eight bells, in this case it is St Mary's in the Market Place.

ROSE AND CROWN   A result of the marriage of Henry VII to Elizabeth of York, daughter of Edward IV, was a great number of *Rose and Crowns*, many still survive.

ROYAL OAK   On the accession of Charles the Second a great number of these sprouted over England. The sign commemorates the escape of the King from Cromwell's Army by hiding in an oak tree.

SEVEN STARS   This was an often quoted astrological sign of the Middle Ages and is shown on sign boards as a constellation, "The Bear", "King Charles' Wain" or the "Plough" as it is often called. An earlier origin before the Reformation was of course from the seven-starred celestial crown worn by the Blessed Virgin in old paintings.

SHOULDER OF MUTTON   Always relates to the second business run from the pub, in this case a butchery business.

SMITHFIELD   Named after the cattle market or Smithfield it adjoined.

TALBOT   Also includes **The Dog** and **Spotted Dog.** The name is of an extinct breed of dog, which was used for hunting. It was white with black or blue spots over the whole body and legs, not unlike the Dalmatian. This name derives from the Earls of Shrewsbury whose family name was Talbot, and is found in places where they had land.

THREE CROWNS   Relates to the union of the crowns of England, Wales and Scotland in 1603. An earlier meaning was the Triple Crown worn by the Bishop of Rome as the head of the Church.

THREE TUNS   The arms of the Vintners' company. A tun was a huge cask of Beer of 252 gallons.

TURKS HEAD   The long struggle of the forces between Christendom and Islam is the reason for this name, as well as names such as **Saracen's Head** or **Moor's Head.** It is an old name and probably relates to an early inn on this site.

VOLUNTEER   Popular in the early 1800s with the local volunteers and militia during the Napoleonic period.

WAGON AND HORSES   Describes the main business of the inn. In this case it stood on Greenhill and for many a long year served the many carriers who plied their business in these parts.

WHEEL   This name was originally **Catherine Wheel** and relates to the martyrdom of St Catherine; the Catherine Wheel symbol was used by the Knights of St Catherine of Mount Sinai, created in the eleventh century for the protection of pilgrims on their way to Jerusalem. The name was popular for an Inn which served travellers. The reformation and the period of the iconoclasts resulted in the reference to the saint being removed and just the name **Wheel** remaining.

WHEATSHEAF   The sign of the Company of Bakers, it is found in all wheat growing counties.

WHITE HART   The most popular sign in the country, it refers to the arms of the Black Prince's son Richard the Second. The origin goes back to Alexander the Great who is supposed to have caught a pure white stag and placed a gold collar around its neck.

WOOLPACK   Relates to the common method of transporting wool in the days when it was the principal business of England.

Alphabetical Index

Continued

O
Old Crown – Bore Street **11**
Old Crown – Tamworth Street **56**
Old Goat's Head–Breadmarket Street **14**
Old Golden Ball-Bore Street **11**

P
Paul Pry – Sandford Street **44**
Pheasant – Beacon Street **21**
Prince of Wales – Bore Street **13**

Q
Queen's Head – Bore Street **13**
Queen's Head – Queen Street **44**

R
Railway Inn – Trent Valley **51**
Railway Tavern – Levetts Field **36**
Red Cow – Greenhill **31**
Red Lion – St John Street **41**
Red Lion – Dam Street **26**
Ring of Bells – Stowe Street **47**
Robin Hood – St John Street **41**
Rose and Crown – Bird Street **17**
Royal Oak – Pipehill **53/54**
Royal Oak – Sandford Street **43**

S
Saddler's Arms – Tamworth Street **55**
Samuels – Market Street **27**
Scales – Market Street **27**
Scott Arms – Dam Street **26**
Seven Stars – Stowe Street **47**
Ship – Sandford Street **44**
Shoulder of Mutton – London Road **34**
Smithfield – Greenhill, Church Street **29**
Spotted Dog – Birmingham Road **19**
Spread Eagle – Greenhill, Church St. **30**
Staffordshire Knot – Stowe Street **48**
Swan Hotel – Bird Street **18**

T
Talbot – Bird Street **17**
Tally Ho – Wade Street **35**
Tankard – Sandford Street **44**
Three Crowns – Breadmarket Street **14**
Three Tuns – Walsall Road **53**
Trent Valley Hotel – Trent Valley **51**
Turf Tavern – Bore Street **13**
Turk's Head – Sandford Street **44**

U
Unicorn – Bird Street **17**

V
Volunteer - Lombard Street **48**

W
Wagon and Horses – Greenhill **32**
Wheatsheaf – Bore Street **18**
Wheel – Beacon Street **22**
White Hart – Greenhill **32**
White Lion – London Road **34**
Windsor Castle – Dam Street **26**
Woolpack – Bore Street **12**

Y
Yew Tree – Old Burton Road **51**

Bibliography

The following works have been consulted in preparing this book:

A Sentimental Journey in and about the Ancient and Loyal City of Lichfield (Alfred Parker) Lomax, Lichfield 1925

Birmingham Pubs (Alan Crawford, Michael Dunn and Robert Thorne) Alan Sutton 1986

Coaching City (Howard Clayton) E.J.Morten, Didsbury, 1976

The Victoria History of the County of Stafford – Vol. XIV Lichfield – Oxford University Press 1990

Victorian Pubs (Mark Girouard) 1975

Quaint Signs of Olde Inns (C.J.Monson-Fitzjohn) Senate 1994

Lichfield Remembered (Cuthbert Brown) Published by the Author 1996

Pigot's Commercial Directory of Staffordshire for 1835 – Pigot, Manchester

History and Gazeteer of Staffordshire for 1834 – White, Sheffield

Typesetting and layout by John Shaw, Lichfield and Printed and Bound by WM Print,
Frederick Street, Walsall, West Midlands,